# Assessing Campus Diversity Initiatives

## A Guide for Campus Practitioners

Mildred García, Cynthia A. Hudgins, Caryn McTighe Musil,
Michael T. Nettles, William E. Sedlacek, and Daryl G. Smith

*This monograph is the third in a series of three publications that are part of AAC&U's project,*
*"Understanding the Difference Diversity Makes: Assessing Campus Diversity Initiatives."*
*AAC&U is grateful to the following organizations for their support: the Ford Foundation,*
*the William and Flora Hewlett Foundation, the James Irvine Foundation,*
*the W.K. Kellogg Foundation, the Lilly Endowment, and the Philip Morris Companies Inc.*

ASSOCIATION OF AMERICAN COLLEGES AND UNIVERSITIES

Washington, D.C.

Published by
the Association of American Colleges and Universities
1818 R Street, NW
Washington, DC 20009
202/387-3760
www.aacu-edu.org

© Copyright 2001

ISBN 0-911696-86-5

*This monograph is one in a series of three publications that are part of AAC&U's project, "Understanding the Difference Diversity Makes: Assessing Campus Diversity Initiatives."*

To order additional copies of this publication or to find out about other AAC&U publications, e-mail pub_desk@aacu.nw.dc.us.

# Contents

## Members of the Diversity Evaluators Collaborative

Mildred García, President, Berkeley College

Cynthia A. Hudgins, Senior Research Associate,
   School of Social Work, University of Michigan

Caryn McTighe Musil, Project Director, Vice President of
   the Office for Diversity, Equity, and Global Initiatives,
   Association of American Colleges and Universities

Michael T. Nettles, Professor of Education, University of Michigan

William E. Sedlacek, Professor of Education and Assistant Director
   Counseling Center, University of Maryland

Daryl G. Smith, Professor of Education and Psychology,
   Claremont Graduate University

## AAC&U Support Staff

Daniel Hiroyuki Teraguchi, Project Manager and Research Associate,
   AAC&U Program Associate, Diversity, Equity, and Global Initiatives,
   1999- Present

Brinton S. Ramsey, Project Manager and Rapporteur, AAC&U Program
   Associate, Diversity, Equity, and Global Initiatives, 1998-1999

Lee Harper, Project Manager and Rapporteur, AAC&U Program Associate,
   Diversity, Equity, and Global Initiatives, 1996-1998

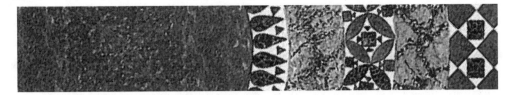

# Acknowledgments

The special challenge for this book's authors was how to make its contents accessible to a wide variety of people on campus wanting to assess their diversity work. At the same time, we needed to promote responsible, credible evaluations whose results would be accurate and useful. Most of those in the writing collaborative were themselves experts in evaluation, comfortable with the discipline's language and concepts, and well trained as statisticians. Only one, despite more than a decade of serving as an evaluator, still felt her strongest identity in her own field, the humanities. Although we take full responsibility for the final words on the pages, the ideas, examples, and inspiration come from many sources. Over the course of the last four years, as we were working simultaneously on crafting all three monographs, we repeatedly consulted with diversity practitioners in the field. They were, among others, faculty members and academic administrators, directors of multicultural affairs, admissions personnel, student affairs staff, and institutional researchers. In forums and conferences, through workshops and emails, they told us what they had learned and what more they needed from us if they were to improve on the campus diversity work to which they were so committed. They identified key stumbling blocks to assessment, contributed strategies, and evaluated various drafts of the monograph as it began to take shape.

We also shared summary drafts of all three monographs with university and college presidents. In a series of roundtable discussions, they shared a set of concerns they had as presidents. These concerns spanned both internal and external audiences and underscored the reality that campus work never takes place in isolation. They also knew full well the kind of educational leadership demanded of them in a world still not at ease with difference, reluctant to fully explore inequalities, and not clear how to mediate the clash of cultures between diverse peoples.

We want to acknowledge with gratitude the five foundations and one corporate philanthropy that invested in the project. We thank the following for their support of this

AAC&U evaluation project: The Ford Foundation, the William and Flora Hewlett Foundation, the James Irvine Foundation, the W.K. Kellogg Foundation, the Lilly Endowment, and the Philip Morris Companies Inc. By investing in campus diversity initiatives, they have helped colleges and universities do a better job of turning diversity into an asset and equality and tolerance into more common campus practice. Moreover, they have helped higher education rethink its definition of academic excellence to include diversity.

We came to know the funding agencies not only as organizations but through the particular program officers with whom we worked directly. It was a privilege and an inspiration to work with such thoughtful, dynamic, and committed people. Dr. Raymond Bacchetti, formerly program officer at the William and Flora Hewlett Foundation, provided distinctive leadership through his foundation's "Pluralism and Unity" initiative; he was a significant influence in conceptualizing and sustaining our diversity evaluation project. He sharpened the edges of our conversations, and his verbal eloquence set a standard for our writing collective. Kitty Breen, formerly education specialist from the Philip Morris Companies Inc., enlivened and warmed our exchanges, reminding us always that understanding how diversity does and doesn't work on campus matters deeply. Her colleague, Diane Eidman, manager of the domestic violence program at Philip Morris, gave continuity to the project. Sam Cargile, formerly program officer of the Lilly Endowment, was there from the beginning, pressing for evaluation language accessible to those not trained in the discipline. Ralph Lundgren of the Lilly Endowment honored Sam's involvement by contributing funds to the project after Sam's departure. Betty Overton-Adkins, former program officer at the W.K. Kellogg Foundation, hosted one of our pre-project planning meetings and helped us craft a clearer purpose for our research. She also demonstrated extraordinary patience and faith when it took longer than anticipated to complete this final publication. Carol Ramsey, formerly of the James Irvine Foundation, immediately understood the importance of the work and its congruence with initiatives at the Irvine Foundation. Author Hughes, also a former program officer at the Irvine Foundation, helped shape our two California presidential roundtables in 1998, hosted both at Irvine's headquarters. Robert Shireman is continuing a proud line of outstanding program officers at Irvine, with a special commitment to deepening the capacities of campuses to evaluate the impact of their diversity work.

Edgar Beckham, former program officer for the Campus Diversity Initiative at the Ford Foundation and now a senior fellow at AAC&U, is, however, in a league of his own. If it were acceptable to list a funder as an author, his name would be the seventh in the writing collaborative. He played a key leadership role throughout the project and was one of the most astute editors of our work. Insistent in prodding our thinking through the five-year process, he queried our findings, pushed at the edges of our initial conceptual certainties, and spurred us on with indefatigable enthusiasm. There wasn't a project meeting he missed or a draft he didn't read and comment on. The prose and organization in the current monograph flows more smoothly because of his pen.

The staff at AAC&U has contributed to this book. Lee Harper, program associate for the first two years of the project and rapporteur of our meetings, made our words sound coherent and, as project manager, made sure the manuscript drafts and people flying all over the country got to the right places at the right time. Brinton Ramsey, program associate for the next two years, plunged right in as if she had been part of the group from the beginning, adding her own expertise in evaluation to improve our thinking and our writing. Finally, our current program and research associate, Daniel Teraguchi has shepherded the final volume to press. His own training as a doctoral student in higher education made him an excellent reader for the manuscript in its newest iteration, and he took care of details with an efficiency and competency that has distinguished him at AAC&U. He was assisted by Michelle Asha Cooper, our newest program associate, who helped with proofing and tracking bibliographic sources. Susan Reiss streamlined the text, and Bridget Puzon, senior editor overseeing all publications, made sure the manuscript met AAC&U's high standards, Ann Kammerer created the striking cover, and Julie Warren saw the text through layout and production, overseen by Suzanne Hyers.

Finally, we are grateful to the students, faculty, staff, and administrators, whose words and work influenced so much of our thinking, at hundreds of campuses involved in campus diversity initiatives. We received regular advice from practitioners over the years who generously gave us feedback on our initial working outlines, fleshed out issues to address, read various drafts, and insisted this was a monograph worth waiting for. We hope we have honored their work and their patience.

A common thread linked all those who informed our work and joined together all the various constituencies who influenced this collaborative project, "Understanding the Difference Diversity Makes": a belief in the importance of evaluation and a conviction that it was critical for those engaged in diversity work to become more systematic in gathering information about outcomes. Too often the very people who know the most about what is happening on campus with college students are too busy to have time to pause to evaluate the programs they invented or oversee. They are at the front lines on a daily, sometimes hourly basis, counseling students in distress, teaching difficult and contentious subject matter in classrooms, supervising students in community partnerships, trying to help underserved students get into college, trying to help those same students stay in college through graduation, working on departmental hiring committees to diversify the faculty, managing a major curriculum change through its complex committees, and running intergroup dialogues in the dorm. It is primarily to that audience that this monograph is directed. We hope it helps give them new insights about their work, suggests pathways for improving upon it, and documents for the wider world the educational and societal value of their efforts.

Mildred García, Berkeley College
Cynthia A. Hudgins, University of Michigan
Caryn McTighe Musil, Association of American Colleges and Universities
Michael T. Nettles, University of Michigan
William E. Sedlacek, University of Maryland
Daryl G. Smith, Claremont Graduate University

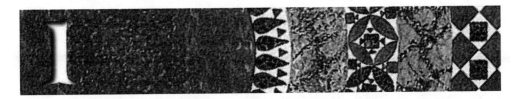

# Introduction

Say the word "assessment" or "evaluation" in a crowded room of college educators and you can predict a hush will follow. Perhaps a collective intake of breath might even be audible. Both the word and the process of assessment frequently trigger a host of negative reactions. Some people are anxious about how to measure changes in learning accurately. Others worry that assessment will be used to undermine their work. Still others are convinced there is simply no way to measure the impact of their efforts. Common to many practitioners is the belief that they just do not have sufficient time to do an evaluation. The authors of this handbook seek to mitigate these concerns by introducing readers to a variety of user-friendly approaches to assessing diversity initiatives.

Drawing on emerging research and proven instruments, we are offering some of the necessary tools needed to evaluate diversity work, whatever one's subject matter or level of expertise in assessment. For the specialist, there are subtle differences between assessment and evaluation. For most people, however, the terms are used interchangeably. We have opted for the purposes of this book to imitate common usage by moving back and forth between the two words as if they were the same thing.

The current volume is one in a series of three monographs published by the Association of American Colleges and Universities (AAC&U) on the topic of diversity in higher education in the United States. The first monograph, *To Form A More Perfect Union: Campus Diversity Initiatives* (1999), draws on research findings that chart a broad array of initiatives at colleges and universities using diversity as an educational resource for all students. It describes principal arguments for addressing diversity, captures the range of activities that comprise campus diversity practice, organizes the emerging national mosaic of campus diversity work into four categories, and underscores the value and significance of assessing diversity work. The second monograph, *A Diversity Research Agenda* (2000), outlines areas of research still needed that will be critically important in shaping the next generation of diversity work. This final monograph, *Assessing Campus Diversity Initiatives*, focuses on the evaluation of diversity efforts.

The three monographs are the product of a collaboration among six scholars—Mildred García, Cynthia A. Hudgins, Caryn McTighe Musil, Michael T. Nettles,

William E. Sedlacek, and Daryl G. Smith. We have worked together over a number of years to pool our experience as evaluators of campus diversity initiatives. Our scholarly work on campus diversity has spanned three decades. It includes developing curricular and co-curricular programs; advising national and state governments; conducting research; and helping colleges and universities, foundations, and corporations assess the effectiveness of their campus diversity initiatives.

Evaluation can improve the educational quality of all students' experiences. It can help an institution know if it is meeting its mission. It can reveal how students across different groups are faring. It can provide blueprints for how and where an institution needs to do better. And it can trumpet the extraordinary progress higher education has made, especially in the last four decades, as it has sought to transform diversity from a problem into a resource.

Telling that story and plotting a course for the future cannot be done without good evaluations. We hope to motivate readers of this handbook to become those storytellers, whether through numbers or narratives, convergent reliability or anecdotal persuasiveness, questionnaires or questioning. Evaluations can demonstrate what works and what requires change. Altering an existing diversity program may be necessary to create one that is more effective.

## A.     Diversity Defined

In this monograph the term "diversity" is most often used to signify a set of campus-based educational activities designed to include students from all backgrounds and to enhance the educational experience of all students. Evidence is mounting that attending to diversity is sound educational practice. It encompasses all domains of institutional life.

Given its particular mission and context, each institution needs to define for itself what it means by diversity. On its face, the term is benign, describing our state as human beings: diverse. But historic practices that have deliberately excluded certain populations, knowledge frameworks, or perspectives from higher education have not been so benign. The consequence of such practices have denied democratic access and stifled or skewed intellectual productivity. Seeking to correct what has come to be understood not only as a civic issue of equal opportunity but an educational one of fully exploring possibilities, institutions have invested in a creative and expansive set of innovative reforms, driven by diversity.

Motivated by the presence of an increasingly diverse student body, the academy, which is more skilled today at capitalizing on that diversity, has now begun to measure the impact of such diversity on learning. The evidence is beginning to suggest that students' cognitive skills are increased by the dissonance of multiple perspectives, their ability to negotiate differences is improved, and their critical thinking skills are sharpened. When exposed to diverse students, courses, and campus environments, students are more likely to recognize inequality when it exists, to engage in remedying it in society, and are more ready to live in racially diverse neighborhoods after they graduate.

Every person who creates, oversees, or participates in diversity programs on campus should also become conversant in how to assess them. Just as diversity in the United States is a mechanism for testing the moral commitments of our democracy, so, too, can evaluation be a measure of testing the educational consequences of diversity.

The ultimate goal of this monograph is to help institutions gather more precise information about the educational consequences and impact of diversity initiatives at their campuses. Which programs are working? What are the results? Which programs are least effective? What adjustments need to be made?

## B.  Using This Handbook

This handbook can be used as a guidebook to the challenging yet invigorating terrain of evaluating campus diversity initiatives. Chapter Two, Evaluation and Diversity, explores the need for assessment and the importance that campus diversity practitioners and administrators should attach to it. Chapter Three, Designing a Campus Diversity Evaluation, presents general concepts and guidelines and identifies various foci of diversity assessment. It also raises questions that diversity practitioners might want to consider as they plan their assessments. The questions are designed to help colleges and universities design their evaluations in the context of institutional history, mission, location, population, and resources, and also to take into account the audiences for whom the assessment is intended. In addition, this chapter considers the range and types of data that may be collected, approaches to data analysis, and various ways findings can be presented.

Chapter Four, Frameworks for Evaluation, concludes the volume by offering some larger frameworks for evaluation, beginning with a discussion of institutional audits and performance indicators that can illuminate the impact of campus practices. For the purposes of this monograph, we have linked these indicators to four dimensions of campus diversity work: 1) access and success, 2) campus climate and intergroup relations, 3) education and scholarship, and 4) institutional viability and vitality. After the discussion of institutional audits, we suggest some existing theoretical models to help frame evaluations.

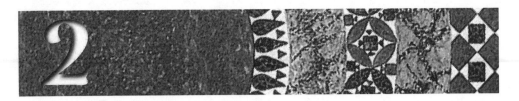

# Evaluation and Diversity

## A.    Why Evaluate?

Evaluations can determine if diversity efforts are successful, if they can be replicated, if they need to be improved or indeed should be abandoned. In addition, assessing diversity can uncover impediments that hamper the academic progress of particular populations. Assessment can also help to identify the positive factors that enhance communication and provide momentum for diversity work.

Evaluations also help communicate the benefits of diversity work to a variety of audiences, some of whom may be skeptical of these efforts. For example, through evaluation we can help a legislator respond to pressure from a white suburban constituency that feels disadvantaged by affirmative admissions and financial aid policies.

Evaluation efforts can win allies within the academy. Faculty members may incorporate more intergroup dialogue in their courses when they see positive evidence of its value emerging from residential life intergroup dialogue. For instance, a skeptical economist may be persuaded that the introduction of diversity materials increases interest in economics and can deepen students' understanding of it. Administrators who may have assigned diversity to specific people or programs may make it central to the overall mission of the college when they see how it enhances learning for all students, including white students.

Evaluation addresses the concerns and questions of the general public. For instance, colleges and universities, both public and private, are increasingly called upon to account for the way they are using resources. Sound evaluation can help institutions predict future costs, but can also demonstrate the benefits that accrue from their investments in diversity.

Evaluation contributes to shaping institutional planning and public policy regarding such issues as admissions, financial aid, faculty recruitment and retention, research, and various kinds of curricular and co-curricular programming. If colleges and universities seek public support for using diversity to achieve academic excellence, they need to assess their efforts and report the outcomes to ensure continuation and expansion of such support.

Evaluation enables practitioners to make necessary adjustments along the way. Evaluating while in the midst of a diversity initiative is especially useful because it can provide information that allows for immediate corrections. For instance, an evaluation may reveal that a campus has succeeded in its goal of increasing the number of racial and ethnic students but not anticipated the ensuing racial tension and competition among different groups. Even though it might not originally have been part of the campus diversity initiative, campus leaders may opt to incorporate new elements into their plan.

Evaluation provides context. As a form of research, it helps us step back from our daily practice and reflect on its relationship to the other relevant activities. Evaluation locates our work in the framework of institutional and national history, such as the financing of higher education and its connection to expanding access.

---

### Why Evaluate?

Evaluation…
- *Produces useful knowledge.*
- *Documents and clarifies diversity work.*
- *Helps to communicate the benefits of diversity work to a variety of audiences.*
- *Addresses the concerns and questions posed by the general public.*
- *Contributes to shaping institutional and broader public policy.*
- *Permits immediate corrections based on results.*
- *Provides context.*

---

## B.     Dimensions and Stages

The expanding number of campus diversity initiatives and the need to assess them can be daunting. Two approaches can frame thinking about campus diversity assessment. The first approach, dimensions of campus diversity, can be thought of as operating in a number of distinct but complementary areas of campus life. The second approach measures progress through Institutional Stages.

### Dimensions of Campus Diversity.
By looking first individually and then relationally at four dimensions listed in figure 1 (opposite page), what and how to evaluate becomes clearer. This framework for

understanding campus diversity was developed by Daryl G. Smith in the book, *Diversity Works: The Emerging Picture of How Students Benefit* (Smith & Associates 1997).

The figure below depicts four interrelated dimensions of campus diversity: access and success, campus climate and intergroup relations, education and scholarship, and institutional viability and vitality. These dimensions can be seen through the lens of the specific groups involved, the campus activities or initiatives focused in the area, the institutional efforts to enhance vitality and viability, and the kinds of questions asked in an evaluation.

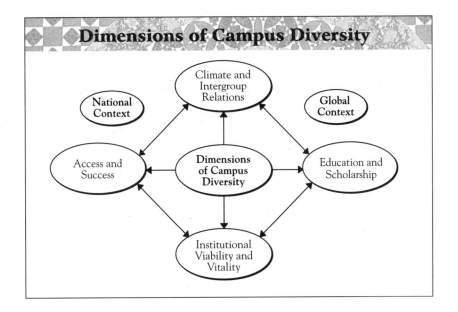

The first dimension, **access and success**, is concerned principally with the inclusion and success of historically underrepresented groups. It focuses on both social justice and education, in that it seeks to redress the historical disadvantage suffered by these groups and also positions them to enhance diversity as an educational resource for all students. Diversity efforts began in this dimension in the mid-1960s and were focused at the outset primarily on historically underrepresented groups identified by race, ethnicity, and gender. Evaluation of access and success has largely been studied through student numbers, representation on campus, representation in relation to some larger population, and graduation/completion rates. Increasingly, researchers are looking at levels of success and achievement across groups. A notable resource in this dimension is Bowen and Bok's book, *The Shape of the River* (1998), which focused on success rates for African-American graduates from selective institutions over time.

The second dimension, **campus climate and intergroup relations**, focuses on the campus environment for historically underrepresented or marginalized groups. This is the dimension in which concern for student welfare was first extended beyond race, ethnicity, and gender to include issues related to sexual orientation, physical ability, and religion. Because of the increasing recognition of the importance of diversity for civic democracy, the focus on creating supportive environments on campus has expanded to include attention to intergroup relations. Attention is given to the multiple ways in which people identify with and participate in groups and the complexity of identities within groups.

Assessment efforts related to climate and intergroup relations often focus on perceptions of the overall climate from the perspective of diverse groups. In addition, evaluation efforts can document patterns and levels of interaction, the conditions under which diverse individuals come together, the multiple and overlapping group memberships that exist, the results of increased interactions, and the effectiveness of a wide variety of programs to improve the climate and intergroup relations on campus.

The third dimension, *education and scholarship*, characterizes the concerns about diversity from the perspective of the educational and scholarly role of the institution. The educational dimension focuses on educating all students to live and function in a pluralistic society and an increasingly linked global community. Scholarship and the curriculum, teaching and learning strategies, recruitment of diverse faculty, and faculty development efforts are the action vehicles in this dimension. Evaluation questions in this dimension might include the following:

- How adequate is the current curriculum and scholarship for educating all students for a pluralistic society and world in terms of *availability* (of courses and activities), *experience* (students' course-taking patterns), and *learning* (impact on the individual student)?
- What teaching and learning strategies serve this purpose?
- How diverse is the faculty, and what difference does this make within departments and the classroom?
- How effective are efforts to deepen faculty engagement with new scholarship related to diversity within and among the disciplines?

Finally, the fourth dimension considers the role of diversity in ensuring *institutional viability and vitality*. This area encompasses the diversity efforts in the other three dimensions and concentrates on the institution as a whole. The focus extends beyond students and beyond scholarship to the institution's own success regarding diversity. Evaluation questions ask:

- How is the institution perceived?
- How do diverse constituencies feel about the institution?
- Is the mission articulated in a manner that is adequate to the diversity aspirations of the first three dimensions? If not, does it need rethinking and restating?
- To what extent is the institution defining itself in terms of the needs of a diverse society?

By probing institutional diversity efforts from another perspective the questions may be framed in the following manner:

- What are the costs of an absence of diversity—for an institution's attractiveness to students, its capacity to market itself, its pursuit of its educational objectives, and its relevance to society?
- What if there is diversity in the student body but not elsewhere in the institution?

Significantly, this dimension focuses attention not just on students but also on the staff and faculty, relationships to important constituencies such as alumni and trustees, institutional mission and planning, and on relationships to communities outside the institution.

Institutional audits are an especially useful example in this sort of evaluation, enabling researchers to capture a profile of the whole institution. Audits can address institutional history as it is perceived by significant constituencies, such as alumni and parents. They can get at perceptions of the institution held by members of the surrounding community. And they can reveal employers' beliefs or perceptions about how effectively students are being prepared to function in a diverse work force.

Audits can also be used to assess the engagement of diversity issues by boards of trustees, to measure population diversity in different sectors and at different ranks, and to gauge the capacity of students to confront diversity issues productively. In addition, comprehensive audits can be used to scrutinize institutional structures and planning processes in their relationship to and impact on the goals of diversity. Some institutions have assembled institutional assessment portfolios as an aid in conducting comprehensive institutional audits (Ingle 1994). An example of an audit framework is described in Chapter Four.

While it is important to scrutinize these dimensions separately, it is equally important to appreciate their interrelationships. Viewed separately, each dimension aids the design of assessments that focus on specific activities. Viewed as a whole the dimensions provide a vision of how each affects every aspect of the institution.

Moving through the various dimensions shifts the focus of evaluation to different groups. *Access*, for example, tends to be the narrowest but most foundational issue. Attention to access typically addresses underrepresented groups, usually previously excluded populations. *Climate* broadens the number of people examined and attends to the interaction between them. All groups at a given campus, including students, faculty, and staff can be evaluated. *Education* widens the scope even further, for it, too, involves everyone but also addresses the fundamental purposes of the academy: What it teaches and toward what ends. Finally, *institutional viability* shifts the evaluative lens to capture the most comprehensive view possible as it investigates the central mission and how it embeds institutional goals in its organizing policies, principles, and procedures on a daily basis, both internally and in the larger world.

### *Measuring Progress through Institutional Stages.*

Another helpful way to begin thinking about evaluation is to examine different stages of institutional development (Richardson, Matthews, and Finney 1992; Sedlacek 1995). While the language of stages can be limiting, it does provide useful metaphors for historical context. It can also complement the language of campus diversity dimensions. A college may be at one stage of development in one dimension of its diversity activities and at another stage in some other dimension. By constructing both stages and dimensions and looking at them reciprocally, an evaluator may achieve a more sophisticated and nuanced understanding of an institution's diversity efforts and avoid the common pitfall of misguided expectations concerning programs and their outcomes.

For heuristic purposes, we can formulate three stages of development (see figure below). Clearly, however, different parts of an institution may be at different stages.

## Stages of Diversity Development

**Stage One**
- Largely homogeneous students, faculty, and staff
- Little attention to campus climate issues
- Modest incorporation of diversity scholarship in the curriculum
- Diversity understood as race alone
- Diversity grafted on to existing structures
- Sporadic rather than coherent diversity plan

**Stage Two**
- Increasing diversity among students, faculty, and staff
- New, but lightly resourced, structures to address diversity issues, typically centered in student affairs
- More attention to climate issues because of new voices on campus
- Diversity understood as more than race
- A catch-all diversity requirement in place with little investment in faculty development
- Diversity courses, but scattered and uneven
- Attempts to coordinate the ad hoc diversity initiatives

**Stage Three**
- Relatively diverse students and staff, but perhaps modest in faculty
- Regular published audits of campus climate
- Well thought-out diversity requirement with more institutional pathways to further study through the majors
- Deeper levels of expertise in faculty and regular opportunities for faculty development
- Range of structures available for diversity research and practice
- Overall institutional plan for integrating diversity into the educational mission and policies
- Emerging partnerships between campus and larger community

The following provide examples of institutions at each stage in its development of diversity.

**Stage One.** A college with little diversity in its student body and faculty and no overall campus diversity plan attempts to add a diversity course to its required first-year curriculum. The president appoints a faculty committee to work out the details but does not invest strong personal leadership in the task. Long-standing battles among academic departments and smoldering tensions among tenured and non-tenured faculty, as well as issues related to "political correctness," dominate the deliberations of the committee for more than a year, and no course is ever formally proposed.

An assessment effort for this institution would focus on the institutional context and other factors that limited success as well as on documentation of the outcome and support for the effort.

**Stage Two.** At this stage of development, there is sufficient diversity at all levels to encourage faculty to share ideas across disciplines. Once a month, faculty with an interest in adding diversity content to their courses come together for a dinner meeting. A member of the faculty with some knowledge of and interest in diversity issues leads the discussions. The administration pays for the dinners, partly out of external grant funds. Faculty learn from one another and teach collaboratively.

An assessment effort at this institution might systematically study the curricular changes introduced and the extent of the changes. The extent of faculty participation, the representation of departments, faculty attitudes toward the program, student enrollments and attitudes, and indicators of student learning outcomes are reasonable targets of inquiry.

**Stage Three.** For an institution at this stage, a key curricular challenge may be coordinating information about the many diversity courses. The university has been developing its diversity work in all four dimensions over a period of many years and is fairly far along in its development. Because there is so much activity in so many areas of campus life, the institution has difficulty assessing the overall impact of diversity on the university as a whole. The challenge for an assessment effort at this stage would be to demonstrate that the change has indeed been institutionally transformative.

Using senior surveys to track student assessments of their educational experience and changes in student attitudes is one technique to aid assessment. Analyzing student transcripts to examine course-taking patterns is another. An institution at the third stage might also consider comprehensive institutional audits involving all four dimensions, along with an institutional assessment portfolio to track progress over time, highlight change, and identify areas requiring continuing effort.

When evaluating any of these stages, it is important that assessment be at the core of the campus diversity initiative rather than an afterthought. At each stage, an evaluation can provide feedback to make necessary developmental changes preparatory to moving to the next stage. In short, assessment should be not at the margins, but a significant element of an institution's campus diversity initiatives.

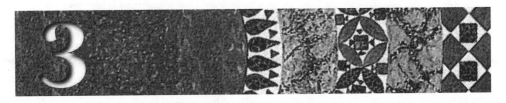

# Designing a Campus Diversity Evaluation

Many practitioners who have never before designed or conducted an assessment hesitate to take on what seems at the outset a Herculean task. However, those who design and conduct evaluations determine the focus of the assessment and can influence the information disseminated from the evaluation's results.

## Ten Steps in Designing Diversity Assessment

STEP ONE:     Define the purpose
STEP TWO:     Determine the audience
STEP THREE: Assemble the evaluation team
STEP FOUR:   Identify the context
STEP FIVE:     Target the topic
STEP SIX:       Formulate the questions
STEP SEVEN: Obtain the data
STEP EIGHT: Assess the data
STEP NINE:     Analyze the data
STEP TEN:       Report the findings

## A.     Step One: Define the Purpose

To guide the initial assessment planning evaluators should be able to answer the following questions:

- Why conduct an evaluation?
- Is it for program improvement? Accountability?
- Does it respond to an institutional mandate?
- Does it fulfill a request or requirement of an external funder?
- Is it to monitor progress?

Evaluations can be thought of in two ways. Formative evaluations are those in which the results are typically used to help administrators strengthen their programs. Summative evaluations are those that look at the results of an effort and produce new knowledge and information for those to whom the administrators are accountable. Summative evaluations are often used for comparing institutions or programs, or simply for keeping track of trends. Much of the same data and information is required for each of the two types of evaluation. Both are equally important, and the audiences for the two frequently overlap. Nevertheless, formative evaluations provide opportunities for feedback to those who are responsible for the diversity program under review, while summative evaluations are often directed at decision makers who may not be as close to the initiative. Both contribute in important ways to institutional or programmatic change and improvement.

## B.      Step Two: Determine the Audience

Clarify the *primary audience* early in the assessment process because it can have direct impact on the evaluation's design, scheduling, language, and final recommendations. Often decision makers are the primary audience. Relevant characteristics of the audience include whether those receiving the results are internal or external to the institution; made up primarily of members of the faculty, the administration, the governing board, or the student body; or include state legislators, the courts, or the general public. Understanding and responding to the questions, concerns, and information needs of various audiences, both in the type of assessment and the mode of dissemination, are essential for gaining support and for addressing central issues.

If an evaluation is developed to respond to an external audience, for instance, it is important to determine what that audience wants to know. It may be primarily interested in the educational impact of the programs and in their societal value. While many funders award grants for specific programs, for example, the programs are usually supported to bring about some deeper change. Both the Ford Foundation and the James Irvine Foundation grant programs on campus diversity, for example, were put into place to foster institutional change. Thus, while assessment of specific programs was relevant, it was not the primary focus. Instead, assessing the impact of the project on the institution was primary. Conducting an evaluation may provide an opportunity to defend a program and to share with the campus and with external communities the program's important achievements. If an administrator or board is concerned about whether some effort is increasing graduation rates, for example, then an evaluation focusing on satisfaction is not adequate.

# C. Step Three: Assemble the Evaluation Team

Consider who will be involved in designing, implementing, and discussing the evaluation. Create a decision-making group that will be responsible for the several phases of the assessment—design, data collection, data analysis, production, and dissemination of reports. To produce the strongest evaluation include multiple perspectives and voices from diverse locations within the institution and from different backgrounds. The team should include some members with experience in assessment and/or with diversity.

Keep in mind that even the best teams experience discord. Develop a tolerance for ambiguity, an ability to respect competing truths, and a recognition that debate and disagreement often lead to new and better insights. By examining the interconnectedness of efforts, the team will identify critical aspects of the initiative under evaluation and how the initiative fits into the larger institution.

# D. Step Four: Identify the Context

At this point consider the institutional context for assessment. What is the environment in which your programmatic or institutional intervention exists? Where did it come from in terms of institutional history?

### Examine the Margin and the Center.

Explore the location of the diversity initiative to be assessed in terms of its distance from what is viewed as the center of the institution. What do the individuals who articulate the institution's mission with the greatest authority think of the initiative or project? At the same time, keep in mind the perspective of those who may be most affected by diversity efforts, but who may not be key decision makers.

In developing an understanding of institutional context, explore each of the following five factors: educational mission, geographic locations, student populations, institutional resources, and pace of change.

**Factors Influencing Diversity**

- Educational Mission
- Regional Location
- Student Populations
- Institutional Resources
- Pace of Change

*Educational mission.* While every college and university has an educational mission, missions change over time, sometimes dramatically. However, they exert powerful influence on governing boards, alumni, and community supporters, as well as students, faculty, and staff. In assessing diversity, it is important to consider how the mission might influence population diversity. Whether an institution is public or private, single-sex or co-educational, secular or sectarian, urban or rural, vocational or liberal arts, two-year or four-year, or founded to serve a particular group will influence its population diversity and shape its commitment to diversity practice. This is true of other institutions, like Hispanic-Serving Institutions, that have altered their original designated student population to serve newly emerging groups. Still others, such as military academies and business colleges, have special educational objectives, all of which will influence an evaluation.

Keep in mind that the mission reaches beyond words. Mission is manifested as well in attitudes and deeds. For example, many colleges and universities in this country advocated the educational desirability and usefulness of diversity well into the second half of the twentieth century, even as they discriminated against various subgroups (women, people of color, religious and ethnic minorities). When inquiring into the relationship between diversity and institutional mission during the design phase of the assessment, it is important to remember not only what the mission statement says but also how it may have come to guide campus planning through the years.

*Regional location.* Regional location can sometimes affect an institution's identity, its relations with its surrounding community, and quite often the demographic profile of its population. In some communities, students of color may be welcome on campus, but shunned or harassed in town. An assessment of campus climate needs to include issues off the campus in addition to concerns on the campus. These issues might concern racial profiling by local police or a lack of knowledge and understanding of diverse cultures among residents. Urban institutions also have diversity challenges often related to stark socioeconomic differences between the campus and the neighboring community. Where the socioeconomic differences correlate with racial differences, they can frustrate many well-meaning attempts to improve campus climate and intergroup relations. Sometimes, a campus responds to its own population diversity in ways that have little relevance to the diversity of the surrounding community, the state in which it is located, or the nation as a whole.

Campus location and regional population demography may also affect an institution's ability to diversify its student body, faculty, and staff, thereby affecting the assessment of goals and success. Some institutions in the Southwest, for example, may have a largely underserved Latino/Latina population, while in California some selective institutions may find their majority student population is Asian American. Developing an understanding of what is an appropriate and desirable mix of students from an ethnic and racial point of view will be very different in New England than in Florida. Indeed, in both regions national numbers may not be useful for comparisons or for setting goals. Different locations demand different strategies.

*Student population.* Mission, geography, and state law may affect the demographic profile of an institution's student body. Some public institutions, for example, are mandated to serve specific geographic counties or regions within a state. Their student populations, then, may necessarily be more limited demographically. Similarly, a private institution with a religious tradition or affiliation may also limit religious diversity. Measuring progress in terms of diversifying a student body must be understood in the context of such mission constraints. Given the broad definitions of diversity, however, difference is omnipresent if not always visible. For instance, in 1995, a consortium of colleges and universities in New Hampshire gathered for a weekend workshop on diversity. Because the state has little racial diversity, they used issues of gender, class, religion, and ethnicity as their entry points for discussing diversity.

*Institutional resources.* The availability of resources is an important consideration when designing diversity assessments. U.S. academic institutions are themselves diverse in their economic resources. Endowments vary widely from institution to institution. State-funded institutions, dependent on state legislatures, often have financial limitations. Many religious institutions, Historically Black Colleges and Universities, women's colleges, and tribal colleges tend to be very small and frequently have modest financial resources. Such limitations can inhibit the kind of progress an institution can make on diversity efforts.

*The pace of change.* Multiple factors affect the speed with which institutions change. Very few institutions have the will, resources, or capacity to move initiatives focused on diversity in every dimension simultaneously. In most colleges and universities, progress is neither uniform nor steady. In some cases, and especially if an institution is new to diversity work, evaluators will have to search carefully for evidence of change. A modest gain in population diversity in a student body or the addition of the first or second faculty member of color may be an occasion for celebration at an institution whose circumstances impede its diversity work.

On the other hand, where diversity efforts have been underway for a longer period of time, diversity evaluators should include in their scrutiny of context the pace and impetus of change. At some institutions change comes in fits and starts, often in response to campus eruptions. At others, movements develop among students or faculty or both. The strength and continuity of these movements influence the pace of change.

At Wesleyan University, for example, a group of liberal, white faculty members who were heavily influenced by the Civil Rights Movement, spurred the institution to its first substantial efforts in support of diversity in the early 1960s. A number of them achieved tenure and remained active into the late 1990s. Their continuing influence helped shape the institution's pursuit of its diversity agenda for more than thirty years.

Multiple factors affect the pace of change. At Wesleyan, some disruptions accelerated change, while others were so debilitating as to require a quiescent period of recovery.

## E.    Step Five: Target the Topic

The next step in designing an assessment is to consider what will be analyzed. Is it the institution? A program or project within the institution? The institution in relation to the larger community? It is important to be clear about what is going to be evaluated and to define boundaries. Without establishing these boundaries, evaluators can fall into the trap of designing an assessment that is unwieldy. Sometimes in trying to answer too many questions, none of them gets adequately answered.

## F.    Step Six: Formulate the Questions

The next crucial step in planning evaluations is to frame the questions. The most important areas for questions may focus on population diversity, campus climate, curricular and co-curricular programs, institutional policies, and related outcomes. The questions that evaluators raise about these matters help to shape the tasks and activities undertaken in assessments. The questions also point toward the possible uses for evaluation findings, and the channels through which findings and recommendations can be disseminated.

The assessment should include basic questions as well as those that will reveal more complex issues. While each program or department will want to frame some unique questions, many questions are generic, particularly for evaluations focusing on the institution. Here are a few sample questions:

1. How successful are we in enrolling a diverse student body and recruiting diverse faculty and administrators?
2. How successful are we in ensuring that students of diverse backgrounds are learning and achieving to their potential?
3. What are all students learning about diversity from our curricular initiatives?
4. How are students benefiting intellectually and socially from campus diversity?
5. How are students of diverse backgrounds interacting with each other?
6. How does campus diversity affect the intellectual life and scholarship of members of the faculty?
7. How does campus diversity contribute to the institution's vitality and viability?
8. How successful has the institution been in reaching diverse constituencies outside the institution?

These broad questions represent a starting place for the kinds of questions that might form an institutional evaluation. Each college and university must also identify the specific questions that are important to address in its own environment.

If the assessment is related to student success and the evaluation looks only at the student and not the institution and its practices, then the results will focus only on the student. By framing the issue so narrowly, institutional practices will be ignored.

Although a standard evaluation instrument geared to answer key questions may exist, avoid changing the team's approach simply to fit a pre-designed assessment by another institution, department, or external source. However, inserting specific contextual questions into an existing instrument may strengthen it because the instrument will then elicit answers not initially addressed by the standard instrument. In the end, the final evaluation designed for a specific campus diversity initiative may be a mosaic of different pieces from a variety of resources, but the best evaluations answer the questions posed by the evaluation team.

## G. Step Seven: Obtain the Data

Much of the data required for assessing campus diversity is available through existing campus administrative databases. Some of the sources for this information include offices of admissions, the registrar, financial aid, human resources, residence life, academic departments, fiscal and administrative affairs, and archives. Further, many colleges and universities have established institutional research offices that serve as the central source/clearinghouse of data and information that are generated in various campus offices. To assess student learning in courses, data already exist in papers, exams, student presentations, grades, journals, and student course evaluations.

Some data will also need to be collected from students, faculty, administrators, and staff through surveys, questionnaires, focus groups, and personal interviews. Off-campus sources often provide data unavailable or unobtainable in any practical way.

### Data mining.

Accessing the data needed for evaluation may require quantitative or qualitative approaches. Evaluators should use whatever techniques work given their audience, the resources available, and the expertise available to carry out the assessment.

Qualitative and quantitative research can complement each other and strengthen the assessment. For instance, a qualitative approach might be geared toward discovering themes and relationships, such as whether students become more open or knowledgeable about race after they enter college. One possible theme that may emerge from qualitative assessments is that white students who have had more cross-racial interaction

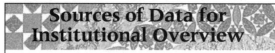

## Sources of Data for Institutional Overview

- Institutional numbers, present and over time
- Graduation numbers overall and by field
- Stop out rates versus dropout rates
- Grades by year and overall
- Honors for diverse groups
- Rates of progress and time to degree data
- Catalogue descriptions
- Faculty development program efforts and faculty participation
- Comparative tenure and promotion rates
- Interviews of department chairs
- Syllabi review
- Transcript evaluation of student course taking
- Freshman surveys of students
- Senior surveys of students
- Climate surveys of all key constituencies
- Donation records by diverse constituencies
- Perceptions of institutional commitment
- Institutional marketing information
- Student newspapers
- Assessments by community partners
- Annual reports

opportunities through student activities and ethnic studies courses also have more open attitudes towards race. Quantitative research can then complement and confirm themes discovered by qualitative methods. By surveying samples and populations, for instance, an instrument might be developed for white students who participated in interracial student organization activities and who enrolled in ethnic studies courses. White students who did not participate can also be surveyed; then the responses can be compared.

However, quantitative assessments may only be useful for some audiences. Often systematic qualitative assessments that reveal accounts of personal encounters or stories about individuals, groups, and circumstances are more valuable. A combination of approaches to gather data may be the most powerful.

Many campus teams begin their assessments with an assumption that a survey should be designed and distributed. Such a decision should come only after it is clear that a survey is the most appropriate method of obtaining the information. Indeed, surveys themselves allow for many different ways of collecting self-reported data—information that can only be collected by and known to the individual. Beyond the standard Likert scale response that assigns a scale value (typically from *strongly agree* to *strongly disagree*) to each response, individuals can be asked to provide written responses, evaluate checklists or inventories, and maintain journal entries for a period of time. Instruments (see Appendices A-E) such as the College Student Experience Questionnaire (CSEQ) and the newly developed National Survey of Student Engagement (NSSE) attempt to develop profiles of student behaviors and use campus resources as ways to investigate learning through behavioral indicators. These surveys also permit comparisons to other institutions through the national data that are collected.

When, however, standard instruments are available, and they have been designed to answer the same kinds of questions that are sought, then it is much wiser to simply adapt them for use. At the same time, finding available sources can be a challenge in itself. From the many efforts undertaken across the country, evaluators can learn a great deal about available instruments and resources. Many campuses are finding the standard instruments, such as those developed by ACT and ETS to be useful for generating attitudinal, behavioral, and performance data. Many prepared instruments permit a campus to add questions for "local use." A number of major universities have developed surveys for their campuses (e.g., annual reports by the University of Michigan on the *Michigan Mandate*); see *Diversity Blueprint*, (1998), which describes the University of Maryland's efforts to institutionalize its diversity efforts. Others have developed ways of assessing student learning through research projects. DiversityWeb, *Studying Diversity in Higher Education*, *Diversity Digest*, and other resources are listed in Appendix F. DiversityWeb (www.diversityweb.org) and *Diversity Digest* (available free in print from the Association of American Colleges and Universities and electronically on DiversityWeb) are rich national compendia of additional information on research and evaluation. Finally, a national Evaluation Tool Kit,

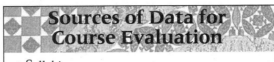

**Sources of Data for Course Evaluation**

- Syllabi
- Catalogue descriptions
- Numbers and kinds of student in class
- Student papers, mid-terms, and final exams
- Student journals, projects, and presentations
- One-minute assessments done periodically
- Student course evaluations
- Comparison of grades across diverse groups of students
- Student portfolios
- Student peer interviews
- Student focus groups
- Alumni surveys

describing many of the available instruments, is being developed through the James Irvine Foundation and will be available on DiversityWeb (www.diversityweb.org).

In addition to surveys, focus groups can be very revealing. Typically, a focus group consists of a discussion with a relatively

**Sources of Data for Summer Bridge Programs**

- Identified areas for improvement
- Evidence of progress in designated area
- Student journals and papers
- Success in college after summer programs
- Retention rates
- Focus group interviews
- Students' perceptions of the value of diversity

small group of people (e.g., 6-10) on a specific topic of interest (e.g., multicultural courses). Participants discuss the issues and an evaluator looks for themes that emerge in the discussions. The primary advantage of focus groups is to obtain more nuanced data from a small number of participants rather than easily quantified but superficial attitudes gained, for instance, through surveys of many individuals. The focus group evaluator can probe for more information and get at subtleties that may be missed in a survey. The primary disadvantage of focus groups is that the participants may not be a statistically representative sample of a particular constituent group (Johnson, Goldberg, and Sedlacek 1995).

Evaluators should embrace creative methods of assessing programs. For example, an approach called "perceptual mapping" has been used to elicit people's feelings about a campus space (Sergent and Sedlacek 1989). African-American students, for instance, have been shown to feel more comfortable than other student groups in spaces where they can develop a sense of community (Sedlacek 1987). Developing a sense of community has in turn been shown to be related to retention, particularly for students of color.

Videotape and audiotape records can also be valuable means of collecting information (assuming that participants have given permission or that anonymity is protected). Observational strategies that investigate patterns of classroom interaction and participation levels in activities can be quite powerful and feasible.

Transcript analysis and catalogue reviews can provide some significant insight into availability of curricular resources and also the degree to which students actually take advantage of these resources. A campus that is looking to assess the impact of curricular transformation projects can use this archival approach to look at the levels of participation rates among both students and faculty, to understand better the characteristics of those who are participating, and to assess the location of diversity efforts. Are diversity courses available in all schools, in major and non-major courses? Are they only taken in response to requirements? Are all appropriate departments involved?

## H.    Step Eight: Assess the Data

Obviously the strength of an assessment depends in large part on the quality of the information obtained. Achieving the best results will be critically important to the assessment's effectiveness and an institution's response to it.

### Getting Good Rates of Return.

Surveys are a fundamental part of many institutional assessments. Student surveys are often weakened, however, not only by a poor return by students overall, but also by small numbers of special populations of students. Where only portions of a student body can be sampled, the evaluator can still include the entire group of students of color, for example, to ensure that the results will be meaningful.

There are several ways to increase rates of return. Attendees of events such as graduation rehearsals or registration can provide responses to periodic surveys. Caution should be exercised, however, when selecting an event so that negativity or its converse do not overwhelm the results. Even providing a free cup of tea or coffee at the snack bar in appreciation for student cooperation can improve the return of surveys. On some campuses and for some purposes, faculty can be enlisted to get responses on instruments or surveys. It is advisable to make sure that the instrument is attractive and that the purpose of the study is clear. In addition, it is necessary to ensure that the survey is not frustrating to complete and that some indication about how the results will be used and shared is given. Response rates of 70 to 80 percent are desirable, though rates of 50 percent are more common.

### Validity and Reliability.

Two terms commonly used by evaluation researchers are "validity" and "reliability." *Validity* refers to the usefulness, appropriateness, and meaningfulness of the assessment. The most important index of validity in the context of diversity may be the assurance that the content assesses what is being asked. It is also important that the content is credible and that the results are not marred by the evaluator's own biases and prejudices.

*Reliability* refers to producing similar results under similar conditions over time. Typically, this can be accomplished by including several measures or judgments about the program or initiatives being assessed. To achieve that, most experts recommend "triangulation," which simply means having multiple angles from which to view a single subject. By using a series of different measures to examine the same thing, convergent validity is established. If, for instance, an assessment measures whether students in a new diversity course understood the interconnections and disconnections between race and gender, three data sets could be examined: student papers, final exam questions designed to elicit analysis of this area, and student journal entries.

Typically, both quantitative and qualitative approaches will include multiple data sets. If, for instance, the campus climate for a particular group is under scrutiny, institutional data on retention rates, a student survey, and a small focus group would be key elements in the assessment. When findings from the various methods converge, stronger, more reliable data are obtained that enable evaluators to make a more persuasive interpretation. If the results do not agree, evaluators can determine where more study is needed to explain discrepancies. An evaluation team at Lewis and Clark College used the matrix below when they were gathering data to assess three key questions they had defined as central to their women's studies program. By mapping an evaluation strategy through this single diagram, one can plot how to proceed, identify logical sources of data, and ensure the use of multiple measurements to verify findings.

| Assessment Matrix for Key Questions at Lewis and Clark College | | | |
|---|---|---|---|
| **Methods Used** | **Q1-Gender Analysis** | **Q2-Institutional Climate** | **Q3-Personal Growth** |
| **Course Evaluations** | X | X | X |
| **Syllabi** | X | **X** | |
| **Computer Conversations** | X | | X |
| **Student Papers** | **X** | **X** | |
| **Symposium Programs** | X | **X** | |
| **Symposium Papers** | X | X | |
| **Questionnaires** **Student** **Alumni** **Faculty** | X X X | **X** **X** **X** | **X** **X** **X** |
| **Journals Diaries** | X | X | X |
| **Honors Projects** | X | X | |
| **Practica** | X | X | X |

* Bold face type indicates primary sources of information for each question.
*Students at the Center: Feminist Assessment* (1992).

# I.    Step Nine: Analyze the Data

Different people need to be involved in analyzing the data. The choice of who will interpret assessment results should be discussed early in the process since it can influence how the data are presented to broader audiences. As previously discussed, different perspectives can provide valuable, new interpretations.

When analyzing the data, it is advisable to be prepared to see trends, points, and issues that may not have been anticipated during the initial assessment design. Such insights offer new avenues to explore.

During the initial analysis, it is most effective to draw only on the data that help illuminate the most fundamental questions in the evaluation. It's easy to become sidetracked by other interesting questions once the analysis begins.

### Interpreting Data from an Inadequate Sample.

Regardless of the best efforts, sometimes data are less than optimal. However, flawed results can be used to construct new and sounder studies that may yield additional insights as the following example shows. At the University of Maryland, the Diversity Evaluation Committee was interested in determining the different ways faculty were involved in diversity activities on campus. Over a five-year period there were six separate studies done on the topic by campus committees, and a dissertation was written on the topic. Each study encountered major methodological problems including unrepresentative samples. However, instead of ignoring the studies, the committee attempted to find some common themes. Six such themes emerged and served as the basis for future evaluation activities. In the new evaluations, multiple measures were utilized to enhance reliability and validity.

### Data Limitations.

Some information may appear useful, but actually may be more isolated and fragmented when scrutinized. For example, much of the information collected in the Lilly Endowment evaluations was anecdotal and consisted of the perceptions of single individuals gathered under conditions where the person providing it may have had reasons to be less than forthcoming. Despite this handicap, these evaluators attempted to measure many things as well as possible, given the task and context. For instance, when only the project director at a Lilly Endowment campus reported that a project had been successful in changing attitudes, the evaluation team sought to corroborate that conclusion from other sources, including interviews with other participants and questionnaire data.

To avoid preconceived methodological limitations, evaluators should concentrate on assessing the climate for diversity rather than on labeling the type of data available as subjective or objective. When working with a single flawed sample or set of data, it is necessary to note limitations but also tease out useful results. However, if the data produce false impressions or make it impossible to answer the questions being posed, one must begin again.

## J.    Step Ten: Report the Findings

After an evaluation is completed, most people hope some changes may come about as a result. In an ideal world, key stakeholders would take one look at the evaluation results, know exactly what to do, and begin to implement change. This is virtually never the case. Below are a number of principles to consider when attempting reforms in response to evaluations.

### Consider the Audience Again.

It is important to revisit the question of audience in this final step. Consider not only the primary audience, but also the secondary audience. Because the evaluation report will likely be disseminated, it is essential to anticipate levels of openness and hostility to the results. There are people who may not be the immediate consumers of the evaluation results but who may receive them, be interested in them, or be helped by them.

### Select the Right Format.

Choose the format to fit a specific audience. Common ways of presenting evaluation results include written reports, distributed internally; reports written for professional publications; oral presentations to classes, seminars, and professional meetings; and reports distributed via e-mail and the Internet. Reports may also be distributed to various media outlets.

The University of Wisconsin at Oshkosh, for example, used social action theater both as a unique program intervention and as a unique means of disseminating evaluation results. Students, faculty, and administrators presented vignettes depicting their evaluation results. They found it to be an effective way of approaching difficult issues. How the theater troupe staged their performances and what issues they chose to depict varied with their audiences.

Students are an important audience for evaluation results. They may be influenced most by their peers, by experiences and observations from their daily curriculum and co-curricular activities, and by issues surrounding the cost and value of their educational experience and credentials. At Colby College in Waterville, Maine, a student theater group proved an effective medium for conveying the diversity evaluation results to a broad, but primarily student audience, through performance on film. Colby commissioned students to assess the climate of race relations on campus. The students used surveys and reviewed historical records in their assessment. The student theater group chronicled the prejudice they had observed and experienced most often in their daily lives on campus.

### Control the Discourse.

Be clear about what the evaluations revealed and what the consequence should be as a result. In this way the evaluators set the parameters of the discourse. Too often, evaluators react defensively to conditions set up by others. By performing an assessment, evaluators gain some power and have the basis from which to persuade those in charge to respond to the results.

For example, at one university, the dean of the college of education was against instituting a course on racism in his college. Evidence from the evaluations of the course content and concern expressed about problems erupting because of unexamined racism convinced the dean of the course's value.

### Become the Source.

By disseminating evaluation results over a period of time, evaluators can earn a reputation as a reliable source of data. Part of being a reliable source is to provide data that address issues of importance, to reflect a methodology appropriate to the questions, and to provide sufficient information so that the audience can trust the conclusions. Always be prepared to share results regardless of the outcome. Posing the right questions and putting them in a context that illuminates remedies enhance the likelihood that data will be used wisely.

### Involve the Critics.

In some cases, it is constructive to involve people who appear to be critical of diversity initiatives in the actual diversity evaluations. They might help identify issues of concern to them as the evaluation questions are determined. They might also be asked to assess some aspects of diversity in areas they oversee. As the results are analyzed, they might be invited to discuss both the results and the appropriate institutional response to the results.

In one external evaluation for the Ford Foundation's *Campus Diversity Initiative*, a group of student leaders from racially defined organizations met with academic and student affairs administrators along with various faculty, including some who had written regularly in campus and local papers about the problems with multiculturalism. The forum allowed everyone to express his or her educational goals, whether as students wanting to achieve or as faculty wanting students to achieve. By the end of the discussion, the once critical faculty had a new understanding about the motives and difficulties of African–American students at the school. The two groups shifted from an oppositional stance to one in which everyone worked together to develop strategies to set high expectations in courses and through student groups for student performance.

### Keep the Analysis Balanced.

Good evaluation measures both the negative and positive impact of a particular diversity program. It is important to avoid the tendency to stress only negative issues in the name of false objectivity. Many opponents of campus diversity try to influence public opinion about campus diversity by stressing the negative. In the long run, shedding light on a topic and calling attention to diversity issues will yield greater gains than limiting access to results and conclusions.

**Possible Formats for Targeted Audiences**

| Format | Target audience |
| --- | --- |
| Detailed report | Faculty |
| Executive summary | Administrators |
| Pamphlet | General public |
| Oral presentation | Classes, seminars, professional meetings |
| Press release | Media outlets |

### Connect with the Overall Institutional Mission.

When formulating ways to implement the results of an evaluation, consider how the results relate to the overall mission of the institution. If an assessment looked at interactivity across groupings and found, as is typical, that the most segregated students on campus are white students, the results could be used to argue for more intergroup contact if white students are to be adequately prepared for living and working in a diverse society and world. If evidence is discovered through evaluations of persistent incidences of individual or systemic racism at a religiously based institution, one might, as one group of evaluators at a Catholic institution did, present the findings as undermining the commitment to racial justice explicitly stated in the school's mission.

When newly implemented anti-affirmative action policies were instituted throughout the California public university and college system, not a single student of color was among the entering freshmen in the University of California, Berkeley School of Law (Boalt Hall). The following year, it was the white law students who protested, insisting that their legal education was diluted because it lacked the dynamic exchange of diverse people from diverse social experiences. The evaluation results from Astin (1993) and Musil (1992) documenting that students who take ethnic and women's studies courses are more engaged as citizens in seeking social justice after graduating can be similarly used to appeal to the standard goal in almost every mission statement of producing graduates who are productive, responsible citizens.

# A Quick Review of the Ten Steps in Evaluation

**Before you begin assessment**

(Steps one through three)

- Consider why you want to conduct an evaluation.
- Clarify who your primary audience is for the results.
- Assemble a diverse and appropriate evaluation team.
- Be sure the process involves diverse campus voices, and give voice to those who may not otherwise be heard.
- Let students participate in the process.

**As you get started**

(Steps four through six)

- Begin where you are as an institution.
- Determine what the most urgent, animating questions are.
- Take time to conceptualize what you want to know.
- Remember to think about the variety of places where education occurs.
- Be clear in your mind that assessment is not final but ongoing.
- Pick a plan you can do.

**Determining the process**

(Steps seven and eight)

- Aim for unobtrusive ways to evaluate.
- Use already existing instruments only if they will answer the questions you determined are the most important for now.
- Rely on data already there or that you can obtain easily.
- Use multiple measures in gathering data.
- Look for alternative ways to do analysis—narrative, conversation, dialogue.

- Think about longitudinal studies: students who graduated, faculty members who have been there a long time, oral histories, and institutional history over time.
- Remember that not all assessment techniques are appropriate to all situations or all institutions.
- Pick and choose among diverse methods, and do what you have time for.

**Analyzing the data** (Step nine)

- Stay focused on your key questions as you analyze the data.
- Return to excess data later as time and staffing permit.
- Interpret data from several viewpoints over time.
- Continue ongoing dialogue with informants, contact people, and constituents.
- Consider assessment as a movie— not a snapshot—with different angles, different cameras, and reviewed over time.

**After the assessment is complete**

(Step ten)

- Review who your primary and secondary audiences are.
- Develop a strategic plan for communicating findings and results.
- Involve students in the disseminating process.
- Anticipate and be prepared for negative reactions to you findings.
- Use a variety of formats to tell your evaluation story.

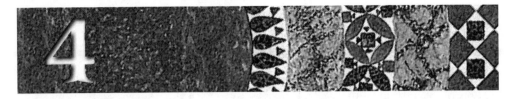

# Frameworks
# for Evaluation

## A.     Institutional Audits

The value of institutional audits derives from several factors. While practitioners at every level should assess the quality and outcomes of their individual projects or activities, it is important to understand the dynamic relationship between a single diversity effort and the status of diversity within the institution as a whole. Institutional audits are an effective way to achieve a comprehensive overview. Hence, many campuses are turning to audits, in some cases as a starting point that provides a benchmark or in others as a result of wanting to measure designated areas of progress against the whole. Audits can be done on a regular basis to mark change or as a means of identifying specific areas to focus upon in greater depth.

Many institutions, no matter how small, can point to a whole range of initiatives related to diversity, and these initiatives are at every stage of development. Often diversity is evaluated by assessing specific interventions or programs. Institutions also evaluate by profiling raw numbers of students, frequently by race and gender. Increasingly, however, institutions are finding it useful to look at diversity in terms of institutional viability and vitality, the fourth among the dimensions of diversity (See Chapter Two, section B). The challenge is to keep such an evaluation manageable. An institutional audit creates a baseline and allows evaluators to measure progress over time. This baseline data can be used comparatively from year to year or even as a means of making a mid-course assessment and formative evaluation.

Institutional audits typically reveal the unevenness in overall progress. An academic dean who has been championing curriculum transformation and supporting faculty development opportunities, for example, might be heartened by tangible evidence of progress. However, improvement in hiring diverse faculty across departments might be negligible. Likewise, there might be evidence of women being more evenly dispersed across business, arts, and humanities, but in the sciences clustered only in biology. An overall audit illustrates both progress and stasis and often suggests strategies for new interventions or priorities for allocating resources.

Because audits provide a larger framework within which to analyze the viability and vitality of the institution, they typically require wider representation across the campus, which in turn brings more diverse people to the table to discuss the results and plan next steps. In all too many institutions, there is no framework to assess the institution and no location for diverse groups to discuss the state of affairs using a comprehensive view. An institutional audit can remedy that situation.

An institutional audit might follow the elements in the box on the following page. The components are organized according to Daryl G. Smith's four dimensions of diversity described in Chapter Two. The best audits are created through broad-based input from a wide range of people and reviewed along the way before final implementation. Each institution, indeed, might begin by agreeing on a core set of indicators in each of the dimensions of diversity to keep things manageable and that can be tracked over time. Managing the audit is key so that the data requirements neither overwhelm nor overburden those attempting to conduct the audit. Such audits, as all good evaluations, rely upon both quantitative and qualitative methods. They will rely mostly on data that already are regularly collected and therefore available. Information for the audit can come from such ready sources as quantitative data collections, evaluation reports, accreditation documents, qualitative interviews and surveys, course evaluations, admissions data, graduation data, and financial records. When creating evaluation tools for each component of the audit, the ten steps of evaluating diversity issues discussed in Chapter Three are useful.

## B.    Models and Theories

It may be useful in some kinds of evaluations to tap the rich body of scholarship that has emerged over the past four decades about various kinds of diverse groups. Although the research was not necessarily designed for evaluative purposes, its theories can often illuminate just the issues being examined in a campus diversity assessment. In some cases, it can even structure the evaluation itself.

Such theories can provide conceptual frameworks for organizing focus groups, analyzing data, or shaping the contents of a survey. There are powerful theories available, for instance, on racial identity development (Helms 1992; Cross 1991; Tatum 1992); on racism models (Sedlacek and Brooks 1976); on intergroup relations (Pettigrew 1980; Zúñiga and Nagda 1992); or on models of bisexual development (Tucker 1995). Other

# Institutional Audit

## Dimension One—Access and Success

Diversity of the undergraduate population, graduate population in fields and levels

Success of students in terms of graduation, persistence, honors, performance

Progress over time in recruiting and retaining traditionally underrepresented students

Diversity of the faculty and staff

Promotion, retention, and tenure rates

## Dimension Two—Campus Climate and Intergroup Relations

Perceptions of the institutional climate

Range of diverse organizations and multiple memberships

Levels and quality of interaction among groups

Quality of experience for diverse groups on campus, in residential life

Levels of use and engagement in a variety of activities, offices, and resources

## Dimension Three—Education and Scholarship

Presence of diversity related courses

Degree to which courses include diversity issues and the location of such courses (general education, electives, and major fields.)

Level of faculty expertise on issues related to diversity

Level of faculty participation in diversity related efforts, diversity of faculty participating

Level of student exposure to diversity courses and diverse faculty

Student learning outcomes

## Dimension Four—Institutional Viability and Vitality

Institutional history with respect to diversity

Progress over time

Perceptions of access, equity, and inclusion from all constituencies

Perceptions of institutional commitment to diversity by all constituencies

Public perception of the institution

Alumni views from diverse groups of alumni

Minority community views of the institution

Economic issues for the institution

Visibility of diversity in publications

Centrality of diversity in the planning process and mission statements available theoretical models examine key diversity issues such as academic achievement (Sedlacek 1994); vulnerability to stereotyping (Steele 1997); achievement models (Treisman 1992); and gender schemas (Valian 1998). There are also more comprehensive institutional overviews of the impact of campus climate on the educational outcomes for different racial/ethnic groups (Hurtado, Milem, Clayton-Pedersen, and Allen 1999).

Sometimes theoretical models can also help an evaluation team see how pieces fit into a wider context. What may be seemingly disconnected bits and pieces in an assessment result may suddenly make sense. For example, at several schools in the Lilly Endowment evaluation, *Improving the Campus Climate for Diversity*, issues related to gays and lesbians kept emerging even though the focus of the assessment was on programs related to African Americans. Until the schools were able to examine the larger issue of prejudice toward any group, they dismissed the findings about gays and lesbians as unrelated. The larger bodies about prejudice gave coherence to the evaluation results and led some schools eventually to develop broader programs dealing with prejudice in general.

The drawback of using models or theories is the risk of forcing results into existing frameworks which may preclude valuable observations and/or limit some measurements to a particular interpretation without examining others. The use of multiple explanatory systems can help avoid this problem. Evaluators may find it useful to discuss this potential pitfall and make concerted efforts to avoid missing unique features of the different programs that might be instructive. Attempts should be made to gather information from the perspective of many individuals at an institution. Having multiple evaluators review the data may also help avoid tunnel vision—forcing results prematurely into a prepackaged model. Evaluators should remain open and willing to change models or theories if the data suggest the logic of doing so. Or data may actually generate an entirely new theory, which may ultimately be useful to others.

### Longitudinal Studies.

Evaluation can be useful in providing an in-depth study of issues over time in a relatively constant manner. Longitudinal studies are especially effective in this way. They typically follow the same people or organizations over time to see how they change. For example, longitudinal studies of students on diversity issues, before and after matriculation, can prove instructive. Bowen and Bok's (1998) exhaustive study in *Shape of the River* is a persuasive example of a longitudinal study. By tracking African Americans who graduated from selective institutions, one of the many elements they were able to document was how this group had become the backbone of the expanded professional class and were deeply engaged in civic activities to strengthen society as a whole.

Longitudinal studies follow the development of students across different races and groups and generate ideas about how to tailor developmental needs by race, culture, and gender. This might in turn lead to a deeper understanding of current student needs. Longitudinal studies are ideal for combining numbers of students, their attitudes, graduation rates, and so on, quantitatively, but also allow qualitative exploration of the stories and issues behind the numbers.

## C.    A Final Note

The aim of this volume is to persuade readers that diversity assessment is valuable and possible, regardless of disciplinary training. Instead of a collective intake of breath when the word "evaluation" is uttered, the monograph should provide tools to design and develop an effective diversity evaluation.

Diversity initiatives that seek to transform institutional mission, campus policies, and educational practices require time and persistence. Evaluating these activities is no different. Evaluations alone cannot bring about change, but dedicated professionals equipped with sound educational goals, rich data, and consistent guiding principles can make a difference. Evaluations, like diversity projects themselves, come in all sizes. Whether the evaluation is a campus-wide climate study or simply an evaluation of a new course, it's the composite picture that matters. (See Jack Meacham's "Assessing Diversity in Courses" in Appendix B). Sometimes, bigger gains can come from a series of smaller interconnected assessment studies. Small victories also tend to attract allies and deter opponents (Weick 1984). Above all it is important to be sure that as many diversity initiatives as possible are evaluated. The cumulative insights gained can help higher education determine whether it is serving its students well and serving society in the process.

According to an important new study *Crossing the Great Divide: Can We Achieve Equity When Generation Y Goes to College?* (2000) by Anthony P. Carnevale and Richard Fry, 2.6 million students will enter college between 1995 and 2015. Of those students, 80 percent will be students of color, a group our nation has a deplorable record of educating well. By 2015, the study predicts 37.2 percent of the entire student population will be minorities. In California, New Mexico, Hawaii, and the District of Columbia, minority students will exceed the percentage of whites. In six others—New York, New Jersey, Maryland, Florida, Louisiana, and Mississippi—the minority population of students will be 40 percent.

As a nation goes to college in the twenty-first century, we need to be ready to teach everyone well so all can thrive. Evaluation is one way to be sure we are doing just that. Our task is to teach a nation—and a world—how diversity can be viewed not as a problem or as a simple gloss on hierarchies, but rather as a valued resource that can help us know more fully, think more wisely, and act more justly.

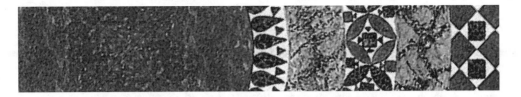

# Bibliography

Astin, A. W. 1993. *What matters in college: Four critical years revisited.* San Francisco, CA: Jossey-Bass.

Bowen, W. and D. Bok. 1999. *The shape of the river: Long-term consequences of considering race in college and university admissions.* Princeton, NJ: Princeton University Press.

Carnevale, A. P. 2000. *Crossing the great divide: Can we achieve equity when Generation Y goes to college?* Princeton, NJ: Educational Testing Service.

Cross, W. E., Jr. 1991. *Shades of black: Diversity in African-American identity.* Philadelphia, PA: Temple University Press.

Helms, J. E. 1992. *A race is a nice thing to have.* Topeka, KS: Content Communications.

Hurtado, S., J.F. Milem, A. R. Clayton-Pedersen, and W. Allen. 1999. Enacting diverse learning environments: Improving the climate for racial/ethnic diversity in higher education. *ASHE-ERIC Higher Education Report* 26:8. Washington, DC: Graduate School of Education and Human Development, The George Washington University.

Ingle, H. T. 1994. Charting campus progress in promoting ethnic diversity and cultural pluralism. In D. G. Smith, L.E. Wolf, and T. Levitan, Eds., *Studying Diversity in Higher Education.* New Directions for Institutional Research, 81. San Francisco, CA: Jossey Bass, 35-51.

Johnson, K. K., J. L. Goldberg, and W. E. Sedlacek. 1995. *Focus groups: A method of evaluation to increase retention of female engineering students.* College Park, MD: Counseling Center, University of Maryland at College Park.

Musil, C. M., ed. 1992. *The courage to question: Women's studies and student learning.* Washington, DC: Association of American Colleges and National Women's Studies Association.

Pettigrew, T. 1980. *The sociology of race relations: Reflection and reform.* New York: Free Press.

Richardson, R., D. Matthews, and B. Finney. 1992. *Improving state and campus environments for quality and diversity: A self assessment.* Denver, CO: Education Commission on the States.

Sedlacek, W. E. 1987. Black students on white campuses: Twenty years of research. *Journal of College Student Personnel* 28:6, 484-95.

Sedlacek, W. E. 1993. Issues in advancing diversity through assessment. *Journal of Counseling and Development* 72, 549-553.

Sedlacek, W. E. 1995. *Improving racial and ethnic diversity and campus climate at four year independent Midwest colleges.* An evaluation report of the Lilly Endowment Grant Program. College Park: University of Maryland.

Sedlacek, W. E. and G. C. Brooks, Jr. 1976. *Racism in American education.* Chicago: Nelson-Hall.

Sergent, M. T., and W. E. Sedlacek 1989. Perceptual mapping: A methodology in the assessment of environmental perceptions. *Journal of College Student Development* 30, 319-322.

Steele, C. M. 1997. A threat in the air: How stereotypes shape the intellectual identities and performance of women and African Americans. *American Psychologist* 52, 613-629.

Smith, D.G. and Associates. 1997. *Diversity works: The emerging picture of how students benefit.* Washington, DC: Association of American Colleges and Universities.

Tatum, B. D. 1992. Talking about race, learning about racism: The application of racial identity development theory in the classroom. *Harvard Educational Review* 62: 1, 1-24.

Treisman, U. 1992. Studying students studying calculus: A look at the lives of minority mathematics students in college. *College Mathematics Journal* 23:5, 362-372.

Tucker, N., ed. 1995. *Bisexual politics: Theories, queries, and visions.* New York, NY: Haworth Press.

University of Maryland, College Park and Association of American Colleges and Universities. 1998. *Diversity blueprint: A planning manual for colleges and universities.* Washington, DC: Association of American Colleges and Universities.

Valian, V. 1998 *Why so slow? The advancement of women.* Cambridge, MA: MIT Press.

Zúñiga, X., and B.A. Nagda. 1992. Dialogue groups: An innovative approach to multicultural learning. In D. Schoem, ed., *Multicultural teaching at the university.* New York, NY: Praeger.

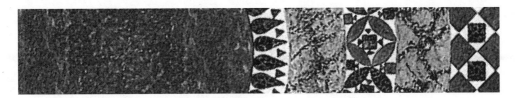

# Appendices

# Appendix A

# CLIMATE, INTERGROUP EXPERIENCE, AND ATTITUDES

The instruments contained in this section represent a range of ways to measure the learning environment for students and their interactions with one another. The results, which can and should be disaggregated by groups, measure how students perceive and feel about a variety of personal and social situations.

The assessment tools* included in this appendix are:

- The Situational Attitude Scale (SAS)
- Cultural Attitudes and Climate at University of Maryland at College Park
- Student's Experiences with Social Diversity at the University of Massachusetts–Amherst
- UNI 100 at Arizona State University

\* All assessment tools are used with permission. Please note that if you decide to use any of the assessment tools, you must obtain a separate copyright permission directly from the author/creator. The copyright holder is listed prior to each tool for your convenience.

# THE SITUATIONAL ATTITUDE SCALE (SAS)

The SAS is a measure of prejudice. Prejudice is defined as some negative attributions or consequences of being a member of a certain group. Measuring the degree of prejudice against a group has been difficult because of the tendency many people have to mask or to avoid expressing such feelings because of social acceptability. In response to this measurement problem, Sedlacek and Brook (1970) developed the SAS. The SAS uses experimental and control forms and provides a situational context to make the psychological withdrawal from the stimulus more difficult. The SAS methodology has been shown to have evidence of reliability and validity in assessing attitudes toward racial and ethnic groups, persons with disabilities, older persons, religious groups, women, children, commuting students, homosexuals, bisexuals, and athletes. This list is not intended to be exhaustive, but only illustrative of some of the groups to which the SAS has been applied.

For more information contact:

William Sedlacek
Professor of Education
Assistant Director, Counseling Center
Adjunct Professor of Pharmacy
1101B Shoemaker Bldg.
University of Maryland
College Park, MD 20742-8111
Phone: 301-314-7687
Email: ws12@umail.umd.edu

## SITUATIONAL ATTITUDE SCALE (SAS)

This questionnaire measures how people think and feel about a number of social and personal incidents and situations. It is not a test, so there are no right or wrong answers. The questionnaire is anonymous, so please DO NOT SIGN YOUR NAME.

Each item or situation is followed by 10 descriptive word scales. Your task is to select, for each descriptive scale, the rating which best describes YOUR feelings toward the item.

Sample item: Starting school this fall

          happy  A  B  C  D  E  sad

You would indicate the direction and extent of your feelings, (e.g., you might select B) by indicating your choice (B) on your response sheet by blackening in the appropriate space for that word scale. DO NOT MARK ON THE BOOKLET. PLEASE RESPOND TO ALL WORD SCALES.

Sometimes you may feel as though you had the same item before on the questionnaire. This will not be the case, so DO NOT LOOK BACK AND FORTH through the items. Do not try to remember how you checked similar items earlier in the questionnaire. MAKE EACH ITEM A SEPARATE AND INDEPENDENT JUDGMENT. Respond as honestly as possible without puzzling over individual items. Respond with your first impression wherever possible.

## SAS
## Form AA

I. You are standing on a very crowded bus surrounded by many people.

| | | | | | | | |
|---|---|---|---|---|---|---|---|
| 1. | fearful | A | B | C | D | E | secure |
| 2. | tolerable | A | B | C | D | E | intolerable |
| 3. | hostile | A | B | C | D | E | indifferent |
| 4. | important | A | B | C | D | E | trivial |
| 5. | conspicuous | A | B | C | D | E | inconspicuous |
| 6. | calm | A | B | C | D | E | anxious |
| 7. | indignant | A | B | C | D | E | understanding |
| 8. | comfortable | A | B | C | D | E | uncomfortable |
| 9. | hate | A | B | C | D | E | love |
| 10. | not resentful | A | B | C | D | E | resentful |

II. You are going on vacation with your best friend and his/her friend of the opposite sex.

| 11. | aggressive | A B C D E | passive |
| 12. | happy | A B C D E | sad |
| 13. | tolerable | A B C D E | intolerable |
| 14. | complimented | A B C D E | insulted |
| 15. | angered | A B C D E | overjoyed |
| 16. | secure | A B C D E | fearful |
| 17. | hopeful | A B C D E | hopeless |
| 18. | excited | A B C D E | unexcited |
| 19. | right | A B C D E | wrong |
| 20. | disgusting | A B C D E | pleasing |

III.    You are boarding a plane for a vacation in Florida, and two young men are boarding immediately behind you.

| 21. | calm | A B C D E | fear |
| 22. | bad | A B C D E | good |
| 23. | safe | A B C D E | unsafe |
| 24. | happy | A B C D E | sad |
| 25. | tense | A B C D E | relaxed |
| 26. | fair | A B C D E | unfair |
| 27. | love | A B C D E | hate |
| 28. | trivial | A B C D E | important |
| 29. | suspicious | A B C D E | trusting |
| 30. | angry | A B C D E | not angry |

IV.    You are buying a used car from a salesman.

| 31. | trust | A B C D E | mistrust |
| 32. | tense | A B C D E | relaxed |
| 33. | fair | A B C D E | unfair |
| 34. | bad | A B C D E | good |
| 35. | happy | A B C D E | sad |
| 36. | comfortable | A B C D E | uncomfortable |
| 37. | clean | A B C D E | dirty |
| 38. | angry | A B C D E | not angry |
| 39. | appropriate | A B C D E | inappropriate |
| 40. | surprised | A B C D E | not surprised |

V.	You are watching a television news program about divorced fathers being given custody of their children.

| 41. | empathy | A B C D E | no empathy |
| 42. | happy | A B C D E | sad |
| 43. | fear | A B C D E | calm |
| 44. | trivial | A B C D E | important |
| 45. | logical | A B C D E | illogical |
| 46. | comfortable | A B C D E | uncomfortable |
| 47. | love | A B C D E | hate |
| 48. | shocked | A B C D E | expected |
| 49. | safe | A B C D E | unsafe |
| 50. | good | A B C D E | bad |

VI.	You are required to attend a religious service for a school research project.

| 51. | fear | A B C D E | calm |
| 52. | strange | A B C D E | natural |
| 53. | sad | A B C D E | happy |
| 54. | good | A B C D E | bad |
| 55. | interesting | A B C D E | uninteresting |
| 56. | logical | A B C D E | illogical |
| 57. | suspicious | A B C D E | not suspicious |
| 58. | bizarre | A B C D E | normal |
| 59. | reasonable | A B C D E | unreasonable |
| 60. | love | A B C D E | hate |

VII.	You notice a student cheating on an exam.

| 61. | expected | A B C D E | unexpected |
| 62. | disgusting | A B C D E | not disgusting |
| 63. | fair | A B C D E | unfair |
| 64. | calm | A B C D E | fear |
| 65. | negative | A B C D E | positive |
| 66. | happy | A B C D E | sad |
| 67. | angry | A B C D E | not angry |
| 68. | normal | A B C D E | not normal |
| 69. | hope | A B C D E | hopeless |
| 70. | shocked | A B C D E | not shocked |

VIII.	You see a group of students staging an on-campus demonstration against discrimination.

| 71. | bad | A B C D E | good |
| 72. | understanding | A B C D E | indifferent |
| 73. | suspicious | A B C D E | trusting |
| 74. | safe | A B C D E | unsafe |
| 75. | disturbed | A B C D E | undisturbed |
| 76. | justified | A B C D E | unjustified |
| 77. | tense | A B C D E | calm |
| 78. | hate | A B C D E | love |
| 79. | wrong | A B C D E | right |
| 80. | humorous | A B C D E | serious |

IX.        You hear of a student getting financial aid.

| 81. | surprise | A B C D E | no surprise |
|-----|----------|-----------|-------------|
| 82. | fair | A B C D E | unfair |
| 83. | reasonable | A B C D E | unreasonable |
| 84. | good | A B C D E | bad |
| 85. | sad | A B C D E | happy |
| 86. | angry | A B C D E | calm |
| 87. | not shocked | A B C D E | shocked |
| 88. | unexpected | A B C D E | expected |
| 89. | positive | A B C D E | negative |
| 90. | serious | A B C D E | not serious |

X.        A new person joins your social group.

| 91. | warm | A B C D E | cold |
|-----|------|-----------|------|
| 92. | sad | A B C D E | happy |
| 93. | superior | A B C D E | inferior |
| 94. | threatened | A B C D E | neutral |
| 95. | pleased | A B C D E | displeased |
| 96. | understanding | A B C D E | indifferent |
| 97. | suspicious | A B C D E | trusting |
| 98. | disappointed | A B C D E | elated |
| 99. | favorable | A B C D E | unfavorable |
| 100. | uncomfortable | A B C D E | comfortable |

101.    Blacken in the appropriate box to indicate your sex

A        Female
B        Male

102.    Blacken in the appropriate box to indicate your age:

A        under 17 years old
B        17 years old
C        18 years old
D        19 years old
E        over 19 years old

103.    The racial or ethnic group to which you belong is:

A        Black (African-American)
B        White (not of Hispanic origin)
C        Asian (Pacific Islander)
D        American Indian (Alaskan native)
E        Hispanic (Latin American)

104.    Are you an Arab or of Arab descent?

A        Yes                B   No

105. Blacken in the appropriate box to indicate your religion or religious preference:

    A    Catholic
    B    Jewish
    C    Protestant
    D    Islamic
    E    Other

106. Blacken in the appropriate box to indicate your father's occupation. Which of the following comes closes to describing your father's occupation? Mark only one answer. If he works on more than one job, mark the most important one. If he is temporarily unemployed, deceased, or if he is retired, mark the one he held last. If your father never held a formal job, leave the item blank.

    A.    Professional — such as clergyman, dentist, doctor, engineer, lawyer, professor, scientist, teacher, etc.

    B.    Semi-professional — such as accountant, airplane pilot, actor, armed forces officer, medical technician, musician, writer, librarian, artist, dental technician, engineering aid, etc.

    C.    Manager–Proprietor-Executive — such as sales manager, store manager, owner of small business, factory supervisor, wholesaler, retailer, contractor, restaurant owner, manufacturer, banker, official in a large company, government official, etc.

    D.    Salesperson — such as life insurance, real estate or industrial goods salesperson, etc.

          Clerical Worker — such as sales clerk, office clerk, bookkeeper, ticket agent, etc.

    E.    Skilled worker or foreperson — such as baker, carpenter, plasterer, electrician, mechanic, plumber, tailor, foreperson, etc.

    F.    Farm or ranch owner or manager.

    G.    Service or Protective — such as armed forces enlistee or non-commissioned officer, barber, beautician, bus driver, fire-fighter, police officer, waiter/waitress, etc.

107. The father's occupation above represents:

    A = full-time work        B = part-time work

108. Mother's occupation - please use the same options found in question 106 to describe your mother's occupation. If your mother never held a formal job, leave the item blank.

109. The mother's occupation described above represents:

    A = full-time work        B = part-time work

## SAS
## Form BA

I.    You are standing on a very crowded bus surrounded
      by many Arab people.

| | | | |
|---|---|---|---|
| 1. | fearful | A  B  C  D  E | secure |
| 2. | tolerable | A  B  C  D  E | intolerable |
| 3. | hostile | A  B  C  D  E | indifferent |
| 4. | important | A  B  C  D  E | trivial |
| 5. | conspicuous | A  B  C  D  E | inconspicuous |
| 6. | calm | A  B  C  D  E | anxious |
| 7. | indignant | A  B  C  D  E | understanding |
| 8. | comfortable | A  B  C  D  E | uncomfortable |
| 9. | hate | A  B  C  D  E | love |
| 10. | not resentful | A  B  C  D  E | resentful |

II.   You are going on vacation with your best friend
      and his/her Arab friend of the opposite sex.

| | | | |
|---|---|---|---|
| 11. | aggressive | A  B  C  D  E | passive |
| 12. | happy | A  B  C  D  E | sad |
| 13. | tolerable | A  B  C  D  E | intolerable |
| 14. | complimented | A  B  C  D  E | insulted |
| 15. | angered | A  B  C  D  E | overjoyed |
| 16. | secure | A  B  C  D  E | fearful |
| 17. | hopeful | A  B  C  D  E | hopeless |
| 18. | excited | A  B  C  D  E | unexcited |
| 19. | right | A  B  C  D  E | wrong |
| 20. | disgusting | A  B  C  D  E | pleasing |

III.  You are boarding a plane for a vacation in Florida and two young Arab men are
      boarding immediately behind you.

| | | | |
|---|---|---|---|
| 21. | calm | A  B  C  D  E | fear |
| 22. | bad | A  B  C  D  E | good |
| 23. | safe | A  B  C  D  E | unsafe |
| 24. | happy | A  B  C  D  E | sad |
| 25. | tense | A  B  C  D  E | relaxed |
| 26. | fair | A  B  C  D  E | unfair |
| 27. | love | A  B  C  D  E | hate |
| 28. | trivial | A  B  C  D  E | important |
| 29. | suspicious | A  B  C  D  E | trusting |
| 30. | angry | A  B  C  D  E | not angry |

IV.      You are buying a used car from an Arab salesman.

| 31. | trust | A B C D E | mistrust |
|-----|-------|-----------|----------|
| 32. | tense | A B C D E | relaxed |
| 33. | fair | A B C D E | unfair |
| 34. | bad | A B C D E | good |
| 35. | happy | A B C D E | sad |
| 36. | comfortable | A B C D E | uncomfortable |
| 37. | clean | A B C D E | dirty |
| 38. | angry | A B C D E | not angry |
| 39. | appropriate | A B C D E | inappropriate |
| 40. | surprised | A B C D E | not surprised |

V.      You are watching a television news program about divorced Arab fathers being given custody of their children.

| 41. | empathy | A B C D E | no empathy |
|-----|---------|-----------|-----------|
| 42. | happy | A B C D E | sad |
| 43. | fear | A B C D E | calm |
| 44. | trivial | A B C D E | important |
| 45. | logical | A B C D E | illogical |
| 46. | comfortable | A B C D E | uncomfortable |
| 47. | love | A B C D E | hate |
| 48. | shocked | A B C D E | expected |
| 49. | safe | A B C D E | unsafe |
| 50. | good | A B C D E | bad |

VI.     You are requred to attend an Islamic religious service for a school research project.

| 51. | fear | A B C D E | calm |
|-----|------|-----------|------|
| 52. | strange | A B C D E | natural |
| 53. | sad | A B C D E | happy |
| 54. | good | A B C D E | bad |
| 55. | interesting | A B C D E | uninteresting |
| 56. | logical | A B C D E | illogical |
| 57. | suspicious | A B C D E | not suspicious |
| 58. | bizarre | A B C D E | normal |
| 59. | reasonable | A B C D E | unreasonable |
| 60. | love | A B C D E | hate |

VII.    You notice an Arab student cheating on an exam.

| 61. | expected | A B C D E | unexpected |
|-----|----------|-----------|------------|
| 62. | disgusting | A B C D E | not disgusting |
| 63. | fair | A B C D E | unfair |
| 64. | calm | A B C D E | fear |
| 65. | negative | A B C D E | positive |
| 66. | happy | A B C D E | sad |
| 67. | angry | A B C D E | not angry |
| 68. | normal | A B C D E | not normal |
| 69. | hope | A B C D E | hopeless |
| 70. | shocked | A B C D E | not shocked |

VIII.    You see a group of Arab students staging an
         on-campus demonstration against discrimination.

| 71. | bad | A B C D E | good |
|---|---|---|---|
| 72. | understanding | A B C D E | indifferent |
| 73. | suspicious | A B C D E | trusting |
| 74. | safe | A B C D E | unsafe |
| 75. | disturbed | A B C D E | undisturbed |
| 76. | justified | A B C D E | unjustified |
| 77. | tense | A B C D E | calm |
| 78. | hate | A B C D E | love |
| 79. | wrong | A B C D E | right |
| 80. | humorous | A B C D E | serious |

IX.    You hear of an Arab student getting financial aid.

| 81. | surprise | A B C D E | no surprise |
|---|---|---|---|
| 82. | fair | A B C D E | unfair |
| 83. | reasonable | A B C D E | unreasonable |
| 84. | good | A B C D E | bad |
| 85. | sad | A B C D E | happy |
| 86. | angry | A B C D E | calm |
| 87. | not shocked | A B C D E | shocked |
| 88. | unexpected | A B C D E | expected |
| 89. | positive | A B C D E | negative |
| 90. | serious | A B C D E | not serious |

X.    A new Arab person joins your social group.

| 91. | warm | A B C D E | cold |
|---|---|---|---|
| 92. | sad | A B C D E | happy |
| 93. | superior | A B C D E | inferior |
| 94. | threatened | A B C D E | neutral |
| 95. | pleased | A B C D E | displeased |
| 96. | understanding | A B C D E | indifferent |
| 97. | suspicious | A B C D E | trusting |
| 98. | disappointed | A B C D E | elated |
| 99. | favorable | A B C D E | unfavorable |
| 100. | uncomfortable | A B C D E | comfortable |

101.   Blacken in the appropriate box to indicate your sex:

       A    Female
       B    Male

102.   Blacken in the appropriate box to indicate your age:

       A    under 17 years old
       B    17 years old
       C    18 years old
       D    19 years old
       E    over 19 years old

103. The racial or ethnic group to which you belong is:

    A    Black (African-American)
    B    White (not of Hispanic origin)
    C    Asian (Pacific Islander)
    D    American Indian (Alaskan native)
    E    Hispanic (Latin American)


104. Are you an Arab or of Arab descent?
    A  Yes                B  No

105. Blacken in the appropriate box to indicate your religion or religious preference:

    A    Catholic
    B    Jewish
    C    Protestant
    D    Islamic
    E    Other

106. Blacken in the appropriate box to indicate your father's occupation.

    Which of the following comes closes to describing your father's occupation? Mark
    only one answer. If he works on more than one job, mark the most important one. If
    he is temporarily unemployed, deceased, or if he is retired, mark the one he held last.
    If your father never held a formal job, leave the item blank.

    A.    Professional — such as clergyman, dentist, doctor, engineer, lawyer, pro-
          fessor, scientist, teacher, etc.

    B.    Semi-professional — such as accountant, airplane pilot, actor, armed
          forces office, medical technician, musician, writer, librarian, artist,
          dental technician, engineering aid, etc.

    C.    Manager-Proprietor-Executive - such as sales manager, store manager,
          owner of small business, factory supervisor, wholesaler, retailer, contrac-
          tor, restaurant owner, manufacturer, banker, official in a large company,
          government official, etc.

    D.    Salesperson — such as life insurance, real estate or industrial goods
          salesperson, etc.

          Clerical Worker — such as sales clerk, office clerk, bookkeeper, ticket
          agent, etc.

    E.    Skilled worker or foreperson — such as baker, carpenter, plasterer, elec-
          trician, mechanic, plumber, tailor, foreperson, etc.

    F.    Farm or ranch owner or manager.

    G.    Service or Protective — such as armed forces enlistee or non-commis-
          sioned officer, barber, beautician, bus driver, fire-fighter, police officer,
          waiter/waitress, etc.

107. The father's occupation above represents:
     A  full-time work          B  part-time work

     Mother's occupation — please use the same options found in question 106 to describe
     your mother's occupation.  If your mother never held a formal job, leave the item
     blank.

109. The mother's occupation described above represents:

     A  full-time work          B  part-time work

# CULTURAL ATTITUDES AND CLIMATE AT
# THE UNIVERSITY OF MARYLAND

This study measures attitudes and beliefs about issues related to racial and ethnic diversity on campus. This survey, designed to study students' perceptions and attitudes towards campus diversity initiatives, is useful to institutions studying their campus climate.

For more information:

William Sedlacek
Professor of Education
Assistant Director, Counseling Center
Adjunct Professor of Pharmacy
1101B Shoemaker Bldg.
University of Maryland
College Park, MD 20742-8111
Phone: 301-314-7687
Email: ws12@umail.umd.edu

# SURVEY OF THE CULTURAL ATTITUDES AND CLIMATE AT MARYLAND

This study examines attitudes and beliefs about issues important to racial and ethnic diversity at the University of Maryland, College Park. Your honest responses are very important in studying these issues on the campus. All responses are anonymous.

**General Instructions:** Read each item carefully and circle or check your response.

## A. Racial and Ethnic Climate

1. Please indicate to what degree you agree with the following statements:

   Strongly Disagree:   1
   Disagree:   2
   Neutral:   3
   Agree:   4
   Strongly Agree:   5
   Not Applicable:   NA

   a. My experiences since coming to UMCP have led me to become more understanding of racial/ethnic differences. . . 1  2  3  4  5  NA

   b. At UMCP getting to know people with racial/ethnic backgrounds different from my own has been easy. . . . . . . . 1  2  3  4  5  NA

   c. My social interactions on this campus are largely confined to students of my race/ethnicity. . . . . . . . . . . . . . . 1  2  3  4  5  NA

   d. At UMCP I feel there are expectations about my academic performance because of my race/ethnicity. . . . . . 1  2  3  4  5  NA

   e. I feel pressured to participate in ethnic activities at UMCP. . 1  2  3  4  5  NA

   f. At UMCP I feel I need to minimize various characteristics of my racial/ethnic culture (e.g. language, dress) to be able to fit in. . . . . . . . . . . . . . . . . . . . . . . . . . . . . . . . . . . . . . . 1  2  3  4  5  NA

   g. My experiences since coming to UMCP have strengthened my own sense of ethnic identity. . . . . . . . . . . 1  2  3  4  5  NA

2. Think about the faculty whose courses you have taken at UMCP. How many of them would you describe as:

None:              1
Few:               2
Some:              3
Most:              4
All:               5
Not Applicable:    NA

a. Approachable outside of the classroom? . . . . . . . . . . . . . . . 1  2  3  4  5  NA

b. Fair to all students regardless of their racial or
   ethnic backgrounds? . . . . . . . . . . . . . . . . . . . . . . . . . . . . . . 1  2  3  4  5  NA

3. Think about your experiences in the classroom. Please
   indicate to what degree you agree with the following statements:

Strongly Disagree:    1
Disagree:             2
Neutral:              3
Agree:                4
Strongly Agree:       5
Not Applicable:       NA

a. In my experience, students of different racial/ethnic backgrounds
   participate equally in classroom discussion and learning. . . 1  2  3  4  5  NA

b. I feel I am expected to represent my race or ethnic
   group in discussions in class. . . . . . . . . . . . . . . . . . . . . . . 1  2  3  4  5  NA

c. Faculty use examples relevant to people of my race/ethnic
   group in their lectures . . . . . . . . . . . . . . . . . . . . . . . . . . 1  2  3  4  5  NA

d. In my classes I feel that my professors ignore my
   comments or questions . . . . . . . . . . . . . . . . . . . . . . . . . . 1  2  3  4  5  NA

4. Please indicate how comfortable you feel in the following situations at UMCP:

Very Uncomfortable: 1
Uncomfortable:      2
Neutral:            3
Comfortable:        4
Very comfortable:   5
Not Applicable:     NA

a. Going to see a faculty member of my own race/ethnicity. . 1  2  3  4  5  NA

b. Speaking with others about my racial/ethnic background. . 1  2  3  4  5  NA

c. Being in situations where I am the only person of my
   racial/ethnic group . . . . . . . . . . . . . . . . . . . . . . . . . . . . . . . 1  2  3  4  5  NA

d. Saying what I think about racial/ethnic issues . . . . . . . . . . 1  2  3  4  5  NA

e. Being with people whose racial/ethnic backgrounds are
   different from my own . . . . . . . . . . . . . . . . . . . . . . . . . . . . 1  2  3  4  5  NA

f. Participating in class. . . . . . . . . . . . . . . . . . . . . . . . . . . . . . 1  2  3  4  5  NA

g. Going to see a faculty member of a different
   race/ethnicity than my own. . . . . . . . . . . . . . . . . . . . . . . . 1  2  3  4  5  NA

h. Being with people whose racial/ethnic backgrounds
   are the same as my own . . . . . . . . . . . . . . . . . . . . . . . . . . . 1  2  3  4  5  NA


## B. How Well Is UMCP Doing on Diversity?

1. The effort made by UMCP to improve relations and understanding between
   people of different racial/ethnic background is:
   ❑ Too little
   ❑ About right
   ❑ Too much
   ❑ Don't know


2. Please indicate to what degree you agree with the following statements:
   Strongly Disagree:    1
   Disagree:             2
   Neutral:              3
   Agree:                4
   Strongly Agree:       5
   Not Applicable:    NA


   a. UMCP has done a good job of providing programs and
      activities that promote multicultural understanding. . . . . . 1  2  3  4  5  NA

   b. At UMCP students are resentful of others whose
      race/ethnicity is different from their own . . . . . . . . . . . . . 1  2  3  4  5  NA

   c. UMCP should have a requirement for graduation that
      students take at least one course on the role of ethnicity
      and race in society . . . . . . . . . . . . . . . . . . . . . . . . . . . . . . 1  2  3  4  5  NA

   d. UMCP does not promote respect for diversity . . . . . . . . . 1  2  3  4  5  NA

e. The *Diamondback's* coverage of racial/ethnic events
and issues is balanced. . . . . . . . . . . . . . . . . . . . . . . . . . . . . . 1  2  3  4  5  NA

f. Diversity at UMCP was one of the reasons
I chose to come here. . . . . . . . . . . . . . . . . . . . . . . . . . . . . . . 1  2  3  4  5  NA

3.  Which racial/ethnic groups should UMCP make special efforts to recruit as
students and as faculty? (please check all that apply)
   ❑ a. Hispanic Americans
   ❑ b. Native Americans
   ❑ c. Asian Americans
   ❑ d. African Americans
   ❑ e. None—no special efforts should be made to recruit
        any particular racial/ethnic group members

## C. General Experience at UMCP

1.  Please indicate to what degree you agree with the following statements:
   Strongly Disagree:     1
   Disagree:              2
   Neutral:               3
   Agree:                 4
   Strongly Agree:        5
   Not Applicable:     NA

   a. UMCP provides an environment for the free and open
   expression of ideas, opinions, and beliefs. . . . . . . . . . . . . . . 1  2  3  4  5  NA

   b. Overall, my educational experience at UMCP has been
   a rewarding one. . . . . . . . . . . . . . . . . . . . . . . . . . . . . . . . . . 1  2  3  4  5  NA

   c. The atmosphere in my classes does not make me
   feel like I belong. . . . . . . . . . . . . . . . . . . . . . . . . . . . . . . . . 1  2  3  4  5  NA

   d. I would recommend UMCP to siblings or friends as a good
   place to go to college. . . . . . . . . . . . . . . . . . . . . . . . . . . . . . 1  2  3  4  5  NA

   e. I feel as though I belong in the UMCP campus community. 1  2  3  4  5  NA

## D. Your Experiences at UMCP

1. Please use the scale below to indicate the extent to which you believe each of the following is present at UMCP

   Little or None:      1
   Some:                2
   Quite a Bit:         3
   A Great Deal:        4
   Not Applicable:      NA

   a. Racial conflict on campus.............................1  2  3  4  5  NA

   b. Respect by faculty for students of different racial
      and ethnic groups.................................1  2  3  4  5  NA

   c. Respect by students for other students of different
      racial and ethnic groups. ...........................1  2  3  4  5  NA

   d. Racial/ethnic separation on campus...................1  2  3  4  5  NA

   e. University commitment to the success of students
      of different racial and ethnic groups...................1  2  3  4  5  NA

   f. Friendship between students of different racial
      and ethnic groups...................................1  2  3  4  5  NA

   g. Interracial tensions in the residence halls. .............1  2  3  4  5  NA

   h. Interracial tensions in the classroom. .................1  2  3  4  5  NA

2. How fairly do you believe you have been treated by the following:

   Very Unfairly:       1
   Unfairly:            2
   Neutral:             3
   Fairly:              4
   Very Fairly:         5
   No Interaction:      NA

   a. University police  ................................1  2  3  4  5  NA

   b. Residence hall personnel   ........................1  2  3  4  5  NA

   c. Faculty  .........................................1  2  3  4  5  NA

   d. Teaching assistants  ..............................1  2  3  4  5  NA

   e. Students  ........................................1  2  3  4  5  NA

3. In each of these settings, to what extent have you been exposed to information about the history, culture, and/or social issues of racial and ethnic groups other than whites?

Not at All:          1
A Little:            2
Some:                3
Quite a Bit:         4
A Great Deal:        5
Not Applicable:    NA

a. In course readings lectures and discussions . . . . . . . . . . . . . 1  2  3  4  5  NA
b. In activities and programs in the residence halls . . . . . . . . 1  2  3  4  5  NA
c. In other university programs or activities . . . . . . . . . . . . . . 1  2  3  4  5  NA
d. In informal interactions and conversations with friends . . 1  2  3  4  5  NA

4. At UMCP how many for-credit courses have you taken from faculty members of the following racial/ethnic groups?
   ❑ a. Hispanic Americans
   ❑ b. Native Americans
   ❑ c. Asian Americans
   ❑ d. African Americans
   ❑ e. Not sure of race/ethnicity of faculty member

5. How many courses have you taken at UMCP that have focused primarily on the culture history or social concerns of:
   a. Racial and ethnic groups (other than whites) in the U.S.?
      Number of Courses: _____
   b. Non-Western racial and ethnic groups outside the U.S.?
      Number of Courses: _____

6. How often do you have difficulty getting help or support from:
Never:               1
Seldom:              2
Sometimes:           3
Often:               4
Not Applicable:    NA

a. Faculty . . . . . . . . . . . . . . . . . . . . . . . . . . . . . . . . . . . . . . . . 1  2  3  4  5  NA
b. Students . . . . . . . . . . . . . . . . . . . . . . . . . . . . . . . . . . . . . . . 1  2  3  4  5  NA
c. Teaching assistants . . . . . . . . . . . . . . . . . . . . . . . . . . . . . 1  2  3  4  5  NA

7. How often have you been exposed to a racist atmosphere created by the faculty?

   Never:              1
   Seldom:             2
   Sometimes:          3
   Often:              4
   Not Applicable:    NA

   a. In the classroom ................................ 1  2  3  4  5  NA
   b. Outside the classroom ........................... 1  2  3  4  5  NA

8. How often have you been exposed to a racist atmosphere created by other students?

   Never:              1
   Seldom:             2
   Sometimes:          3
   Often:              4
   Not Applicable:    NA

   a. In the classroom ................................ 1  2  3  4  5  NA
   b. Outside the classroom ........................... 1  2  3  4  5  NA

9. Please indicate whether your experience at UMCP has changed your behavior in any of the following ways:

   a. I now recognize culturally biased behavior
      I had not previously identified.              ❑ Yes   or   ❑ No

   b. I now discuss topics related to cultural awareness
      with friends.                                 ❑ Yes   or   ❑ No

   c. I now stop myself from using language that may be
      offensive to others.                          ❑ Yes   or   ❑ No

   d. I now handle negative language used by another in
      such a way as to try to educate the other person.   ❑ Yes   or   ❑ No

   e. I now initiate contact with people who are not of
      my culture or ethnic background.              ❑ Yes   or   ❑ No

## E. Diversity Initiative Programs

1. Have you heard about the University of Maryland
   Diversity Initiative?                    ❑ Yes   or   ❑ No

2. Have you attended or participated in any programs sponsored by the Diversity
   Initiative on campus this year? (These programs include such titles as Diversity
   Research Forum, Improving Communication Between & Within Student
   Groups, and International House Coffee Hour). ❑ Yes   ❑ No   ❑ Don't Know

3. To what degree do you agree that attending programs on diversity contributes to
   the Diversity Initiative's goal of building community?
   ❑ Strongly Disagree
   ❑ Disagree
   ❑ Neutral
   ❑ Agree
   ❑ Strongly Agree
   ❑ Not Applicable

## F. Your Intentions for the Future

1. Do you plan to return to UMCP next semester
   (Summer or Fall 1995)?                 ❑ Yes   ❑ No   ❑ Don't Know

2. If you do not return to UMCP, do you think you
   will transfer to another college or university?   ❑ Yes   ❑ No   ❑ Don't Know
   Please indicate your current college:
   ❑ Agriculture
   ❑ Health and Human Performance
   ❑ Architecture
   ❑ Human Ecology
   ❑ Arts and Humanities
   ❑ Journalism
   ❑ Behavioral and Social Sciences
   ❑ Letters and Sciences
   ❑ Business and Management
   ❑ Library and Information Sciences
   ❑ Computer Math and Physical Sciences
   ❑ Life Sciences
   ❑ Education
   ❑ School of Public Affairs
   ❑ Engineering
   ❑ Undergraduate Studies

3. Please indicate your cumulative GPA at UMCP:
- ❑ 3.5 - 4.0
- ❑ 3.0 - 3.4
- ❑ 2.5 - 2.99
- ❑ 2.0 - 2.49
- ❑ below 2.0

4. Please indicate your current place of residence:
- ❑ University residence hall
- ❑ Fraternity or sorority house
- ❑ Off-campus rental housing/apartment
- ❑ Home of parents or relatives
- ❑ Own home
- ❑ Other (please specify) _____

a. Please tell us what you think UMCP could do differently to improve campus climate with regard to diversity.

Thank you very much for completing this survey. Your efforts will help the University of Maryland, College Park to provide a quality education to its students.

# STUDENTS' EXPERIENCE WITH SOCIAL DIVERSITY AT THE UNIVERSITY OF MASSACHUSETTS–AMHERST

This survey was part of larger project that investigated students' engagement with social diversity at the University of Massachusetts - Amherst. The survey uncovers information about inter-group interaction, communicating across differences, and perspectives and beliefs about conflict and social justice. This study seeks to affirm diversity, cultivate leadership, and build community to positively impact student engagement with diversity in living and learning contexts.

For more information contact:

Ximena Zúñiga
Assistant Professor
Social Justice Education Program
School of Education
University of Massachusetts - Amherst
383 Hills South
Amherst, MA 01003
Phone: 413-545-0918
Email: xzuniga@educ.umass.edu

# Students' Experiences with Social Diversity - Fall 2000

*This survey is part of a larger research project that investigates UMass students' experiences with social diversity. Your responses to this questionnaire are completely confidential, and will be examined only after being grouped with those of other students. Please answer the questions as honestly and accurately as possible. Your name will not be associated with your responses. We ask for your Student I.D. number in order to do a subsequent "follow-up" study. Your cooperation in this important research project is greatly appreciated.*

**INSTRUCTIONS:** Please use a pencil or pen and fill in the oval completely to indicate your response. Avoid making any stray marks on the form, and erase cleanly any stray marks.

**Right** ○ ○ ○ ○      **Wrong** ○ ○ ○ ○

**Are you:** ○ Female ○ Male

**Citizenship Status:**

○ U.S. Citizen
○ Permanent U.S. Resident
○ Neither

**Religious Affiliation:**

○ Buddhist
○ Greek Orthodox
○ Hindu
○ Jewish
○ Moslem
○ Protestant
○ Roman Catholic
○ None
○ Other _____

**Are you a person with a disability?**      ○ Yes      ○ No

**If YES, please mark all that apply:**

○ Physical disability
○ Learning disability
○ Other _____

**Which of the following BEST describes your race or ethnicity?**

○ Bi-racial or Multi-racial
○ African-American or Black
○ Asian-American or Pacific Islander
○ Latino/Hispanic
○ Native American or Alaskan Native
○ White or European-American
○ Cape Verdean
○ Other _____

**How old are you?**

[grid of ovals 0-9, two columns]

**Are you a:**

○ First year student
○ Sophomore
○ Junior
○ Senior

**What is your sexual orientation?**

○ Heterosexual
○ Lesbian
○ Gay
○ Bisexual

**What residence hall do you live in this Fall semester?**

○ Gorman
○ Wheeler
○ Kennedy
○ Other _____

**For how many semesters have you lived in this residence hall (not including Fall 2000) ?**

○ None
○ One
○ Two
○ Three
○ Four
○ Five
○ Six
○ Seven
○ Eight
○ Nine
○ Ten or more

**Which of the following best describes your socio-economic status?**

○ Lower class
○ Lower middle class
○ Middle class
○ Upper middle class
○ Upper class
○ Other _____

**If you were NOT born in the U.S., for how many years have you lived in this country?**

[grid of ovals 0-9, two columns]

**How would you describe the racial/ethnic composition of each of the following:**

All or Nearly All White
Mostly White
Half White and Half Non-White
Mostly Non-White
All or Nearly All Non-White

the neighborhood where you grew up? ○○○○○

the high school you attended? ○○○○○

your friends on this campus? ○○○○○

your friends in general? ○○○○○

**Was English the primary language spoken in your home when you were growing up?**

○ Yes
○ No

**If not, what was the primary language?**

_____

**Please indicate your nine-digit Student I.D. number.**

| ⓪ | ⓪ | ⓪ | ⓪ | ⓪ | ⓪ | ⓪ | ⓪ | ⓪ |
| ① | ① | ① | ① | ① | ① | ① | ① | ① |
| ② | ② | ② | ② | ② | ② | ② | ② | ② |
| ③ | ③ | ③ | ③ | ③ | ③ | ③ | ③ | ③ |
| ④ | ④ | ④ | ④ | ④ | ④ | ④ | ④ | ④ |
| ⑤ | ⑤ | ⑤ | ⑤ | ⑤ | ⑤ | ⑤ | ⑤ | ⑤ |
| ⑥ | ⑥ | ⑥ | ⑥ | ⑥ | ⑥ | ⑥ | ⑥ | ⑥ |
| ⑦ | ⑦ | ⑦ | ⑦ | ⑦ | ⑦ | ⑦ | ⑦ | ⑦ |
| ⑧ | ⑧ | ⑧ | ⑧ | ⑧ | ⑧ | ⑧ | ⑧ | ⑧ |
| ⑨ | ⑨ | ⑨ | ⑨ | ⑨ | ⑨ | ⑨ | ⑨ | ⑨ |

**How often have you experienced each of the following?**

| | Never | Rarely | Sometimes | Often |
|---|---|---|---|---|
| Socialized with someone of a different race/ethnicity. | ○ | ○ | ○ | ○ |
| Socialized with someone of a different sexual orientation. | ○ | ○ | ○ | ○ |
| Socialized with someone of a different religion. | ○ | ○ | ○ | ○ |
| Studied with other students. | ○ | ○ | ○ | ○ |
| Dined with someone from a different racial/ethnic group. | ○ | ○ | ○ | ○ |
| Studied with someone from a different racial/ethnic group. | ○ | ○ | ○ | ○ |
| Dated someone. | ○ | ○ | ○ | ○ |
| Dated someone from a different racial/ethnic group. | ○ | ○ | ○ | ○ |
| Dated someone of a religion different from your own. | ○ | ○ | ○ | ○ |
| Participated in ethnic or cross cultural activities or organizations. | ○ | ○ | ○ | ○ |

**For the following statements, think about situations in which you are discussing social issues with people from DIFFERENT racial/ethnic, gender, sexual orientation, or other social groups. Please indicate the extent to which you agree or disagree with each statement.**

| | Strongly Disagree | Somewhat Disagree | Neither Agree nor Disagree | Somewhat Agree | Strongly Agree |
|---|---|---|---|---|---|
| I am able to express myself when discussing controversial issues. | ○ | ○ | ○ | ○ | ○ |
| I feel comfortable asking people of OTHER races/ethnicities about their perspectives on racial issues. | ○ | ○ | ○ | ○ | ○ |
| I feel threatened when others challenge my opinions or feelings on issues. | ○ | ○ | ○ | ○ | ○ |
| I feel comfortable talking about gay/lesbian issues with people of different sexual orientations. | ○ | ○ | ○ | ○ | ○ |
| I value the opportunity to examine social issues in SMALL GROUP settings. | ○ | ○ | ○ | ○ | ○ |
| I am able to challenge others' opinions when I feel they are misinformed. | ○ | ○ | ○ | ○ | ○ |
| I think people's personal experiences help shed light on the impact of social issues. | ○ | ○ | ○ | ○ | ○ |
| I learn the most about social issues in discussions with my PEERS. | ○ | ○ | ○ | ○ | ○ |

For the following statements, think about situations in which you are discussing social issues with people from DIFFERENT social groups (e.g. racial/ethnic, gender, sexual orientation or other). Please indicate how well each statement describes you.

|  | Not at all like me | A little bit like me | Somewhat like me | Quite a bit like me | Very much like me |
|---|---|---|---|---|---|
| I sometimes find it difficult to see things from the other person's point of view. | ○ | ○ | ○ | ○ | ○ |
| I have learned from my contact with lots of people that no one group has "the truth" or knows "the right way to live." | ○ | ○ | ○ | ○ | ○ |
| If I am sure about something, I don't waste much time listening to other people's arguments. | ○ | ○ | ○ | ○ | ○ |
| It is important for me to educate others about the social group(s) to which I belong. | ○ | ○ | ○ | ○ | ○ |
| I try to look at everybody's side of a disagreement before I make a decision. | ○ | ○ | ○ | ○ | ○ |
| I think a lot about the influence that society has on people. | ○ | ○ | ○ | ○ | ○ |
| I like to learn about social group(s) different from my own. | ○ | ○ | ○ | ○ | ○ |
| I really enjoy finding out about the reasons or causes for people's opinions and behaviors. | ○ | ○ | ○ | ○ | ○ |
| I think a lot about the influence that society has on my thoughts, feelings, and behaviors. | ○ | ○ | ○ | ○ | ○ |
| I want to bridge differences between different social groups. | ○ | ○ | ○ | ○ | ○ |
| I believe there are many sides to every issue and try to look at most of them. | ○ | ○ | ○ | ○ | ○ |
| When I analyze a person's behavior, I often find that causes are linked to a chain of events that go back in time. | ○ | ○ | ○ | ○ | ○ |

**How often have you had a discussion about race/ethnicity with someone from another racial/ethnic group?**

- ○ Never
- ○ Rarely
- ○ Sometimes
- ○ Often

**If you HAVE had such discussions, have they been...**

- ○ Nearly all positive experiences
- ○ More positive than negative experiences
- ○ Mixed equally between positive and negative experiences
- ○ More negative than positive experiences
- ○ Nearly all negative experiences

**How often have you had a discussion about sexism with a person of the opposite sex?**

- ○ Never
- ○ Rarely
- ○ Sometimes
- ○ Often

**If you HAVE had such discussions, have they been...**

- ○ Nearly all positive experiences
- ○ More positive than negative experiences
- ○ Mixed equally between positive and negative experiences
- ○ More negative than positive experiences
- ○ Nearly all negative experiences

We are all members of different social groups (for example, gender, race, ethnicity, sexual orientation, physical or mental ability, socio-economic class, religion, and age). Some of these may seem more important or relevant to you than others. The following questions ask how you experience yourself and others in relation to these various social groups.

**How OFTEN do you think about your:**

| | Never | Rarely | Sometimes | Often |
|---|---|---|---|---|
| Gender | ○ | ○ | ○ | ○ |
| Race | ○ | ○ | ○ | ○ |
| Ethnicity | ○ | ○ | ○ | ○ |
| Sexual orientation | ○ | ○ | ○ | ○ |
| Physical or mental ability | ○ | ○ | ○ | ○ |
| Socio-economic class | ○ | ○ | ○ | ○ |
| Religion | ○ | ○ | ○ | ○ |
| Age | ○ | ○ | ○ | ○ |

**Have you personally experienced or witnessed harassment or discrimination based on any of the following?  (MARK ALL THAT APPLY)**

| | Experienced | Witnessed |
|---|---|---|
| Religious affiliation | ○ | ○ |
| Sexual orientation | ○ | ○ |
| Socio-economic class | ○ | ○ |
| Sex | ○ | ○ |
| Race/Ethnicity | ○ | ○ |
| Other | ○ | ○ |
| (please specify)_____ | | |

Please indicate how accurately the statements below reflect your thoughts and feelings about conflict.

|  | Not at all like me | A little bit like me | Somewhat like me | Quite a bit like me | Very much like me |
|---|---|---|---|---|---|
| I am afraid of conflicts when discussing social issues. | ○ | ○ | ○ | ○ | ○ |
| I believe that conflict and disagreements enrich the learning process. | ○ | ○ | ○ | ○ | ○ |
| I believe conflict almost always ends up with one side winning and the other side losing. | ○ | ○ | ○ | ○ | ○ |
| I believe conflicts between different social groups rarely have positive consequences. | ○ | ○ | ○ | ○ | ○ |
| I think that conflicts between social groups can help clarify misunderstandings. | ○ | ○ | ○ | ○ | ○ |
| I have learned that the best thing is to avoid conflict. | ○ | ○ | ○ | ○ | ○ |
| I believe that conflict is a normal part of life. | ○ | ○ | ○ | ○ | ○ |
| I believe conflict between groups makes it difficult for people to communicate with each other. | ○ | ○ | ○ | ○ | ○ |

Please indicate how likely you would be to take each of the following actions.

|  | Very Unlikely | Somewhat Unlikely | Somewhat Likely | Very Likely |
|---|---|---|---|---|
| Challenge others on racially/sexually derogatory comments. | ○ | ○ | ○ | ○ |
| Join an organization that promotes cultural diversity. | ○ | ○ | ○ | ○ |
| Organize an educational program to inform others about social issues. | ○ | ○ | ○ | ○ |
| Make efforts to educate yourself about other groups(e.g. ethnic groups, genders, sexual orientations). | ○ | ○ | ○ | ○ |
| Challenge others who make jokes that are derogatory to any group. | ○ | ○ | ○ | ○ |
| Call or write to protest when a newspaper or T.V. show perpetuates or reinforces a bias or prejudice. | ○ | ○ | ○ | ○ |
| Make efforts to get to know individuals from diverse backgrounds. | ○ | ○ | ○ | ○ |
| Get together with others to challenge discrimination. | ○ | ○ | ○ | ○ |
| Refuse to participate in jokes that are derogatory to any group. | ○ | ○ | ○ | ○ |
| Recognize and challenge biases that affect your own thinking. | ○ | ○ | ○ | ○ |
| Avoid using language that reinforces negative stereotypes. | ○ | ○ | ○ | ○ |

This survey is part of a larger research project that investigates UMass students' experiences with social diversity. Your responses to this questionnaire are completely confidential, and will be examined only after being grouped with those of other students. Please answer the questions as honestly and accurately as possible. Your name will not be associated with your responses. We ask for your Student I.D. number in order to do a subsequent "follow-up" study. Your cooperation in this important research project is greatly appreciated.

INSTRUCTIONS: Please use a pencil or pen and fill in the oval completely to indicate your response. Avoid making any stray marks on the form, and erase cleanly any stray marks.

Right ○ ○ ○ ○　　Wrong ○ ○ ○ ○

Throughout this past academic year, how many hours per week did you spend participating in each of the items listed below?

| 0 | 1-2 | 3-5 | 6-10 | 11+ | HOURS PER WEEK |
|---|-----|-----|------|-----|----------------|
| ○ | ○ | ○ | ○ | ○ | Recreation / sports / exercise |
| ○ | ○ | ○ | ○ | ○ | Working for pay (on & off campus) |
| ○ | ○ | ○ | ○ | ○ | Ethnic / cultural activities |
| ○ | ○ | ○ | ○ | ○ | Academic clubs |
| ○ | ○ | ○ | ○ | ○ | Arts / media (e.g. music, dance, theater, painting) |
| ○ | ○ | ○ | ○ | ○ | Religious / spiritual involvement |
| ○ | ○ | ○ | ○ | ○ | Fraternity / sorority activities |
| ○ | ○ | ○ | ○ | ○ | Socializing with friends |
| ○ | ○ | ○ | ○ | ○ | Governmental / political involvement |
| ○ | ○ | ○ | ○ | ○ | Student-run business |
| ○ | ○ | ○ | ○ | ○ | Volunteer work |
| ○ | ○ | ○ | ○ | ○ | Other organized activities not listed above |

Please indicate the number of times you participated in each TYPE of activity IN YOUR RESIDENCE HALL this academic year.

| 0 | 1 | 2-3 | 4-6 | 7+ | TIMES THIS ACADEMIC YEAR |
|---|---|-----|-----|-----|--------------------------|
| ○ | ○ | ○ | ○ | ○ | Socials |
| ○ | ○ | ○ | ○ | ○ | Recreational (e.g. intramural sports, Tae Bo) |
| ○ | ○ | ○ | ○ | ○ | Cultural programs (e.g. talent show, cultural dinner) |
| ○ | ○ | ○ | ○ | ○ | Health & personal development (e.g. stress management, yoga, safe sex workshop) |
| ○ | ○ | ○ | ○ | ○ | Community meetings (e.g. House Council, floor meetings, building-wide meetings) |
| ○ | ○ | ○ | ○ | ○ | Social awareness programs (e.g. AIDS awareness, sexual assault awareness, racial / ethnic issues) |
| ○ | ○ | ○ | ○ | ○ | Spiritual / religious (e.g. Bible study group, meditation workshop) |
| ○ | ○ | ○ | ○ | ○ | Performing arts (e.g. art exhibit, a capella concert) |
| ○ | ○ | ○ | ○ | ○ | Safety, violence prevention (e.g. alcohol & violence workshop, residence hall safety, self-defense) |
| ○ | ○ | ○ | ○ | ○ | Academic & career development (e.g. resume writing, study groups) |
| ○ | ○ | ○ | ○ | ○ | Volunteer work (e.g. work at survival centers or shelters) |

**Compared to the beginning of this academic year how would you describe your:**

| | Great improvement | Some improvement | Little improvement | No improvement |
|---|---|---|---|---|

|  | | | | |  | | | | |
|---|---|---|---|---|---|---|---|---|---|
| Social self-confidence | ○ | ○ | ○ | ○ | Ability to think critically | ○ | ○ | ○ | ○ |
| Time management skills | ○ | ○ | ○ | ○ | Leadership skills | ○ | ○ | ○ | ○ |
| Ability to address conflicts between people | ○ | ○ | ○ | ○ | Ability to get along with people of different races / ethnicities | ○ | ○ | ○ | ○ |
| Intellectual self-confidence | ○ | ○ | ○ | ○ | Understanding of social inequities | ○ | ○ | ○ | ○ |
| Understanding yourself | ○ | ○ | ○ | ○ | Abillity to work cooperatively | ○ | ○ | ○ | ○ |
| Ability to work in diverse groups | ○ | ○ | ○ | ○ | Academic achievement | ○ | ○ | ○ | ○ |
| Public speaking skills | ○ | ○ | ○ | ○ | Emotional health | ○ | ○ | ○ | ○ |
| Understanding of problems facing your campus community | ○ | ○ | ○ | ○ | Ability to take responsibility for your own learning | ○ | ○ | ○ | ○ |
| Interpersonal skills | ○ | ○ | ○ | ○ | Drive to achieve | ○ | ○ | ○ | ○ |
| Problem solving skills | ○ | ○ | ○ | ○ | Understanding of others | ○ | ○ | ○ | ○ |

**How often have you experienced each of the following?**

| | Never | Rarely | Sometimes | Often |
|---|---|---|---|---|
| Socialized with someone of a different race/ethnicity. | ○ | ○ | ○ | ○ |
| Socialized with someone of a different sexual orientation. | ○ | ○ | ○ | ○ |
| Socialized with someone of a different religion. | ○ | ○ | ○ | ○ |
| Studied with other students. | ○ | ○ | ○ | ○ |
| Dined with someone from a different racial/ethnic group. | ○ | ○ | ○ | ○ |
| Studied with someone from a different racial/ethnic group. | ○ | ○ | ○ | ○ |
| Dated someone. | ○ | ○ | ○ | ○ |
| Dated someone from a different racial/ethnic group. | ○ | ○ | ○ | ○ |
| Dated someone of a religion different from your own. | ○ | ○ | ○ | ○ |
| Participated in ethnic or cross-cultural activities or organizations. | ○ | ○ | ○ | ○ |

**For the following statements, think about situations in which you are discussing social issues with people from DIFFERENT racial/ethnic, gender, sexual orientation, or other social groups. Please indicate the extent to which you agree or disagree with each statement.**

| | Strongly Disagree | Somewhat Disagree | Neither Agree nor Disagree | Somewhat Agree | Strongly Agree |
|---|---|---|---|---|---|
| I am able to express myself when discussing controversial issues. | ○ | ○ | ○ | ○ | ○ |
| I feel comfortable asking people of OTHER races/ethnicities about their perspectives on racial issues. | ○ | ○ | ○ | ○ | ○ |
| I feel threatened when others challenge my opinions or feelings on issues. | ○ | ○ | ○ | ○ | ○ |
| I feel comfortable talking about gay/lesbian issues with people of different sexual orientations. | ○ | ○ | ○ | ○ | ○ |
| I value the opportunity to examine social issues in SMALL GROUP settings. | ○ | ○ | ○ | ○ | ○ |
| I am able to challenge others' opinions when I feel they are misinformed. | ○ | ○ | ○ | ○ | ○ |
| I think people's personal experiences help shed light on the impact of social issues. | ○ | ○ | ○ | ○ | ○ |
| I learn the most about social issues in discussions with my PEERS. | ○ | ○ | ○ | ○ | ○ |

**For the following statements, think about situations in which you are discussing social issues with people from DIFFERENT social groups (e.g. racial/ethnic, gender, sexual orientation or other). Please indicate how well each statement describes you.**

| | Not at all like me | A little bit like me | Somewhat like me | Quite a bit like me | Very much like me |
|---|---|---|---|---|---|
| I sometimes find it difficult to see things from the other person's point of view. | ○ | ○ | ○ | ○ | ○ |
| I have learned from my contact with lots of people that no one group has the "truth" or knows "the right way to live." | ○ | ○ | ○ | ○ | ○ |
| If I am sure about something, I don't waste much time listening to other people's arguments. | ○ | ○ | ○ | ○ | ○ |
| It is important for me to educate others about the social group(s) to which I belong. | ○ | ○ | ○ | ○ | ○ |
| I try to look at everybody's side of a disagreement before I make a decision. | ○ | ○ | ○ | ○ | ○ |
| I think a lot about the influence that society has on people. | ○ | ○ | ○ | ○ | ○ |
| I like to learn about social group(s) different from my own. | ○ | ○ | ○ | ○ | ○ |
| I really enjoy finding out about the reasons or causes for people's opinions and behaviors. | ○ | ○ | ○ | ○ | ○ |
| I think a lot about the influence that society has on my thoughts, feelings, and behaviors. | ○ | ○ | ○ | ○ | ○ |
| I want to bridge differences between different social groups. | ○ | ○ | ○ | ○ | ○ |
| I believe there are many sides to every issue and try to look at most of them. | ○ | ○ | ○ | ○ | ○ |
| When I analyze a person's behavior, I often find that causes are linked to a chain of events that go back in time. | ○ | ○ | ○ | ○ | ○ |

**Please indicate your nine-digit Student I.D. number.**

[grid of bubbles 0–9 in nine columns]

**Which of the following BEST describes your race or ethnicity?**

- ○ Bi-racial or Multi-racial
- ○ African-American or Black
- ○ Asian-American or Pacific Islander
- ○ Latino / Hispanic
- ○ Native American or Alaskan Native
- ○ White or European-American
- ○ Cape Verdean
- ○ Other

**Compared with the beginning of this academic year, how would you NOW describe the importance that each of the following has to you personally?**

| | Much less important | Less important | Unchanged | More important | Much more important |
|---|---|---|---|---|---|
| Raising awareness about hate crimes | ○ | ○ | ○ | ○ | ○ |
| Helping to promote economic equality | ○ | ○ | ○ | ○ | ○ |
| Raising awareness about rape and sexual assault on campus | ○ | ○ | ○ | ○ | ○ |
| Helping to promote equality based on sexual orientation | ○ | ○ | ○ | ○ | ○ |
| Becoming involved in programs to clean up the environment | ○ | ○ | ○ | ○ | ○ |
| Helping to promote racial / ethnic equality | ○ | ○ | ○ | ○ | ○ |
| Helping to promote gender equality | ○ | ○ | ○ | ○ | ○ |
| Becoming a community leader | ○ | ○ | ○ | ○ | ○ |
| Participating in a community action project | ○ | ○ | ○ | ○ | ○ |
| Becoming involved in my residence hall community | ○ | ○ | ○ | ○ | ○ |
| Doing volunteer work | ○ | ○ | ○ | ○ | ○ |

**How many credits have you taken this academic year?**

[grid of bubbles 0–9, two columns]

**In how many of your courses this year was the PRIMARY focus on racial / ethnic, cultural or gender issues?**

[grid of bubbles 0–9, two columns]

**What residence hall do you live in this semester?**

- ○ Gorman
- ○ Wheeler
- ○ Kennedy
- ○ Other

**Are you:**

- ○ Female
- ○ Male

**Have you heard of Project Mosaik?**

- ○ Yes
- ○ No

**How involved have you been in Project Mosaik activities / courses?**

- ○ Very involved
- ○ Somewhat involved
- ○ Somewhat uninvolved
- ○ Very uninvolved

We are all members of different social groups (for example, gender, race, ethnicity, sexual orientation, physical or mental ability, socio-economic class, religion, and age). Some of these may seem more important or relevant to you than others. The following questions ask how you experience yourself and others in relation to these various social groups.

How OFTEN do you think about your:

Have you personally experienced or witnessed harassment or discrimination based on any of the following? (MARK ALL THAT APPLY)

| | Never | Rarely | Sometimes | Often | | Experienced | Witnessed |
|---|---|---|---|---|---|---|---|
| Gender | ○ | ○ | ○ | ○ | Religious affiliation | ○ | ○ |
| Race | ○ | ○ | ○ | ○ | Sexual orientation | ○ | ○ |
| Ethnicity | ○ | ○ | ○ | ○ | Socio-economic class | ○ | ○ |
| Sexual orientation | ○ | ○ | ○ | ○ | Sex | ○ | ○ |
| Physical or mental ability | ○ | ○ | ○ | ○ | Race/Ethnicity | ○ | ○ |
| Socio-economic class | ○ | ○ | ○ | ○ | Other | ○ | ○ |
| Religion | ○ | ○ | ○ | ○ | (please specify)_____ | | |
| Age | ○ | ○ | ○ | ○ | | | |

**Please indicate how accurately the statements below reflect your thoughts and feelings about conflict.**

Scale: Not at all like me / A little bit like me / Somewhat like me / Quite a bit like me / Very much like me

| | Not at all like me | A little bit like me | Somewhat like me | Quite a bit like me | Very much like me |
|---|---|---|---|---|---|
| I am afraid of conflicts when discussing social issues. | ○ | ○ | ○ | ○ | ○ |
| I believe that conflicts and disagreements enrich the learning process. | ○ | ○ | ○ | ○ | ○ |
| I believe conflict almost always ends up with one side winning and the other side losing. | ○ | ○ | ○ | ○ | ○ |
| I believe conflicts between different social groups rarely have positive consequences. | ○ | ○ | ○ | ○ | ○ |
| I think that conflicts between social groups can help clarify misunderstandings. | ○ | ○ | ○ | ○ | ○ |
| I have learned that the best thing is to avoid conflict. | ○ | ○ | ○ | ○ | ○ |
| I believe that conflict is a normal part of life. | ○ | ○ | ○ | ○ | ○ |
| I believe conflict between groups makes it difficult for people to communicate with each other. | ○ | ○ | ○ | ○ | ○ |

**Please indicate how likely you would be to take each of the following actions.**

Scale: Very Unlikely / Somewhat Unlikely / Somewhat Likely / Very Likely

| | Very Unlikely | Somewhat Unlikely | Somewhat Likely | Very Likely |
|---|---|---|---|---|
| Challenge others on racially / sexually derogatory comments. | ○ | ○ | ○ | ○ |
| Join an organization that promotes cultural diversity. | ○ | ○ | ○ | ○ |
| Organize an educational program to inform others about social issues. | ○ | ○ | ○ | ○ |
| Make efforts to educate yourself about other groups (e.g. ethnic groups, genders, sexual orientations). | ○ | ○ | ○ | ○ |
| Challenge others who make jokes that are derogatory to any group. | ○ | ○ | ○ | ○ |
| Call or write to protest when a newspaper or T.V. show perpetuates or reinforces a bias or prejudice. | ○ | ○ | ○ | ○ |
| Make efforts to get to know individuals from diverse backgrounds. | ○ | ○ | ○ | ○ |
| Get together with others to challenge discrimination. | ○ | ○ | ○ | ○ |
| Refuse to participate in jokes that are derogatory to any group. | ○ | ○ | ○ | ○ |
| Recognize and challenge biases that affect your own thinking. | ○ | ○ | ○ | ○ |
| Avoid using language that reinforces negative stereotypes. | ○ | ○ | ○ | ○ |

# UNI 100 STUDENT SURVEYS
# AT ARIZONA STATE UNIVERSITY

Housed in the Division of Undergraduate Academic Services, UNI 100, Academic Success at the University, is a 3-hour elective course designed to help freshmen and sophomores at ASU adjusting to and succeeding at the university. Each semester, the enrolled students are surveyed to measure their attitudes and experiences. For example, campus leaders can attain useful data regarding demographics, student satisfaction, student involvement, and student experiences. In addition, information concerning students feelings and perceptions about faculty-student relations, peer relations, racial integration/discrimination, and institutional commitment to issues of diversity can be ascertained. This ongoing analysis helps to focus continual campus improvements.

For more information on UNI 100:

Leslie A. Chilton
Department of English
Arizona State University
Tempe, AZ   85287-0302
Phone:  480-965-9257
Email:  smo1407@ASU.EDU

# UNI 100 Survey

In keeping with ASU s commitment to Excellence in Undergraduate Education, we are asking how you evaluate and perceive this course, as well as initial experiences at ASU, future plans, and expectations. Please complete all items on this survey and respond as honestly as possible. Responses will be confidential and will be reported only as group data.

**Section I**

A. How satisfied were you with each of the following aspects of UNI 100?
   (Circle one response for each item)

|    |               | Very Satisfied | Satisfied | Dissatisfied | Very Dissatisfied |
|----|---------------|:----:|:----:|:----:|:----:|
| 1. | Content       | 1 | 2 | 3 | 4 |
| 2. | Assignments   | 1 | 2 | 3 | 4 |
| 3. | Textbook      | 1 | 2 | 3 | 4 |
| 4. | OVERALL course | 1 | 2 | 3 | 4 |

B. Evaluate your UNI 100 *instructor* by responding to the following items. (Circle one response for each item)

| The instructor | | Almost Always | Usually | Occasionally | Almost Never |
|----|-------------------------------------------------|:----:|:----:|:----:|:----:|
| 1. | was prepared for class | 1 | 2 | 3 | 4 |
| 2. | had meaningful/worthwhile lessons | 1 | 2 | 3 | 4 |
| 3. | communicated ideas clearly and effectively | 1 | 2 | 3 | 4 |
| 4. | was available for assistance outside of class | 1 | 2 | 3 | 4 |
| 5. | showed interest in the subject | 1 | 2 | 3 | 4 |
| 6. | showed interest in the students | 1 | 2 | 3 | 4 |
| 7. | used approaches that stimulated student interest | 1 | 2 | 3 | 4 |
| 8. | responsibly handled class discussions/student | 1 | 2 | 3 | 4 |
| 9. | related theoretical material to its practical application | 1 | 2 | 3 | 4 |
| 10. | had a good balance of lecture, activities, and discussion | 1 | 2 | 3 | 4 |
| 11. | was fair and impartial with grading | 1 | 2 | 3 | 4 |
| 12. | clearly explained grading procedures | 1 | 2 | 3 | 4 |
| 13. | made course expectations clear to students | 1 | 2 | 3 | 4 |
| 14. | used exams which covered course material | 1 | 2 | 3 | 4 |

C. Circle one response for each of the two items below.

|    |                                          | Very Difficult | Difficult | N/A | Easy | Very Easy |
|----|------------------------------------------|:----:|:----:|:----:|:----:|:----:|
| 1. | *Before* taking UNI 100, I expected it to be | 1 | 2 | 3 | 4 | 5 |
| 2. | *After* taking UNI 100, I believe it was | 1 | 2 | 3 | 4 | 5 |

D. What did you find (a) most and (b) least useful about UNI 100?

   (a)  Most useful:_____

   (b)  Least useful:_____


E. What did you find (a) most and (b) least helpful about your instructor s teaching?

   (a)  Most helpful: _____

   (b.)  Least helpful: _____


F. Below are expectations you might have had about what UNI 100 would be like or be about or help you learn. Make TWO judgments (**see A & B**) for each expectation, using the scales to the right of each item.

| | A. How important was each expectation in influencing your decision to take UNI? | | | | | B. How much did UNI 100 meet your expectations? | | | | |
|---|---|---|---|---|---|---|---|---|---|---|
| Expectation | Critical | Much | Some | Little | None | Very Much | Much | Some | Little | None |
| 1. Gain a better understanding of myself | 1 | 2 | 3 | 4 | 5 | 1 | 2 | 3 | 4 | 5 |
| 2. Develop my own set of values & ethical standards | 1 | 2 | 3 | 4 | 5 | 1 | 2 | 3 | 4 | 5 |
| 3. Develop my study skills | 1 | 2 | 3 | 4 | 5 | 1 | 2 | 3 | 4 | 5 |
| 4. Develop awareness of people and values from outside of US | 1 | 2 | 3 | 4 | 5 | 1 | 2 | 3 | 4 | 5 |
| 5. Develop appreciation for civic & community involvement | 1 | 2 | 3 | 4 | 5 | 1 | 2 | 3 | 4 | 5 |
| 6. Learn to withhold judgment, ask questions & examine other views | 1 | 2 | 3 | 4 | 5 | 1 | 2 | 3 | 4 | 5 |
| 7. Develop my test-taking skills | 1 | 2 | 3 | 4 | 5 | 1 | 2 | 3 | 4 | 5 |
| 8. Easy grade | 1 | 2 | 3 | 4 | 5 | 1 | 2 | 3 | 4 | 5 |
| 9. Develop my research skills | 1 | 2 | 3 | 4 | 5 | 1 | 2 | 3 | 4 | 5 |
| 10. 3-hour course credit | 1 | 2 | 3 | 4 | 5 | 1 | 2 | 3 | 4 | 5 |
| 11. Have someone I can go to if I have any questions or problems during my first semester at ASU | 1 | 2 | 3 | 4 | 5 | 1 | 2 | 3 | 4 | 5 |
| 12. Learn about services on campus | 1 | 2 | 3 | 4 | 5 | 1 | 2 | 3 | 4 | 5 |
| 13. Meet other students from my major with whom I can study | 1 | 2 | 3 | 4 | 5 | 1 | 2 | 3 | 4 | 5 |
| 14. Meet other students with whom I can socialize | 1 | 2 | 3 | 4 | 5 | 1 | 2 | 3 | 4 | 5 |
| 15. Learn about expectations and logistics of college courses | 1 | 2 | 3 | 4 | 5 | 1 | 2 | 3 | 4 | 5 |
| 16. Learn how to get more involved in campus activities | 1 | 2 | 3 | 4 | 5 | 1 | 2 | 3 | 4 | 5 |

G.  Complete BOTH parts (A & B) for each item below.
    (A)  First, complete the sentence to indicate whether or not you have done each activity
         **since you started at ASU.**
    (B)  Second, indicate whether you think you might get involved in each activity in the next six months or so.

| *Have you….* | A. Have done this | | B. Plan to do this | |
|---|---|---|---|---|
| | **No** | **Yes** | **No** | **Yes** |
| 1.  Talked with faculty informally outside of class | 1 | 2 | 1 | 2 |
| 2.  Voiced an opinion about a controversial issue(s) | 1 | 2 | 1 | 2 |
| 3.  Personally sought information which addresses issues of diversity | 1 | 2 | 1 | 2 |
| 4.  Become personally involved in a discussion/debate with someone whose race/ethnicity differs from your own | 1 | 2 | 1 | 2 |
| 5.  Participated in a student study group on your own initiative outside of class | 1 | 2 | 1 | 2 |
| 6.  Made friends with students whose academic/major interests differs from yours | 1 | 2 | 1 | 2 |
| 7.  Praised, encouraged, or defended someone for his or her views on a topic | 1 | 2 | 1 | 2 |
| 8.  Attended an info. session, talk, or meeting which addresses issues of diversity such as race/ethnicity, women s issues, sexual orientation, etc. | 1 | 2 | 1 | 2 |
| 9.  Participated in serious discussions with students whose religious beliefs, life philosophies, or personal values differ from your own | 1 | 2 | 1 | 2 |
| 10. Given advice, information, or assistance to someone whose race/ethnicity differs from your own | 1 | 2 | 1 | 2 |
| 11. Gotten advice, information, or assistance from someone whose race/ethnicity differs from your own | 1 | 2 | 1 | 2 |
| 12. Used the library as a place to study and/or do research for classes | 1 | 2 | 1 | 2 |

H.  How good were the following aspects of your UNI 100*course?*

| | Very Good | Good | Average | Poor | Very Poor |
|---|---|---|---|---|---|
| 1.  Overall quality of the ***course*** | 1 | 2 | 3 | 4 | 5 |
| 2.  Overall quality of ***instructor*** | 1 | 2 | 3 | 4 | 5 |
| 3.  Classmates, as contributors to the quality of the class | 1 | 2 | 3 | 4 | 5 |
| 4.  Yourself, as a contributor to the quality of the class | 1 | 2 | 3 | 4 | 5 |
| 5.  Overall climate toward discussion and learning | 1 | 2 | 3 | 4 | 5 |

   5a. Why do you describe the climate this way? _____

**Section II**

A.  How would you characterize the *racial/ethnic climate* at ASU on the following dimensions?
    (Circle one response for each )

| | | | | Neutral | | | |
|---|---|---|---|---|---|---|---|
| 1. | Tense | 1 | 2 | 3 | 4 | 5 | Relaxed |
| 2. | Hostile | 1 | 2 | 3 | 4 | 5 | Friendly |
| 3. | Intolerant | 1 | 2 | 3 | 4 | 5 | Tolerant |
| 4. | Uncomfortable | 1 | 2 | 3 | 4 | 5 | Comfortable |
| 5. | Socially separate | 1 | 2 | 3 | 4 | 5 | Socially integrated |

B. How would you characterize the climate at ASU in terms of *gender (male/female) relations?*
(Circle one response for each)

| | | | | Neutral | | | |
|---|---|---|---|---|---|---|---|
| 1. | Tense | 1 | 2 | 3 | 4 | 5 | Relaxed |
| 2. | Hostile | 1 | 2 | 3 | 4 | 5 | Friendly |
| 3. | Intolerant | 1 | 2 | 3 | 4 | 5 | Tolerant |
| 4. | Uncomfortable | 1 | 2 | 3 | 4 | 5 | Comfortable |
| 5. | Socially separate | 1 | 2 | 3 | 4 | 5 | Socially integrated |

C. How would you characterize the climate at ASU for people of differing *sexual orientation?*
(Circle one response for each)

| | | | | Neutral | | | |
|---|---|---|---|---|---|---|---|
| 1. | Tense | 1 | 2 | 3 | 4 | 5 | Relaxed |
| 2. | Hostile | 1 | 2 | 3 | 4 | 5 | Friendly |
| 3. | Intolerant | 1 | 2 | 3 | 4 | 5 | Tolerant |
| 4. | Uncomfortable | 1 | 2 | 3 | 4 | 5 | Comfortable |
| 5. | Socially separate | 1 | 2 | 3 | 4 | 5 | Socially integrated |

D. How would you characterize the climate at ASU for people of differing *religious groups?*
(Circle one response for each)

| | | | | Neutral | | | |
|---|---|---|---|---|---|---|---|
| 1. | Tense | 1 | 2 | 3 | 4 | 5 | Relaxed |
| 2. | Hostile | 1 | 2 | 3 | 4 | 5 | Friendly |
| 3. | Intolerant | 1 | 2 | 3 | 4 | 5 | Tolerant |
| 4. | Uncomfortable | 1 | 2 | 3 | 4 | 5 | Comfortable |
| 5. | Socially separate | 1 | 2 | 3 | 4 | 5 | Socially integrated |

**Section III**
A. Since you've been at ASU, how often have you heard a *fellow student* make insensitive or disparaging remarks about…

| | | Never | 1 or 2 Times | 3-5 Times | 6-9 Times | $\geq$ 10 Times |
|---|---|---|---|---|---|---|
| 1. | Men | 1 | 2 | 3 | 4 | 5 |
| 2. | Women | 1 | 2 | 3 | 4 | 5 |
| 3. | Racial/ethnic minorities | 1 | 2 | 3 | 4 | 5 |
| 4. | Gay, lesbian, bisexual persons | 1 | 2 | 3 | 4 | 5 |
| 5. | Disabled persons | 1 | 2 | 3 | 4 | 5 |
| 6. | Non-native English speakers | 1 | 2 | 3 | 4 | 5 |
| | Persons of certain religious backgrounds | 1 | 2 | 3 | 4 | 5 |

B.  Since you've been at ASU, how often have you heard a *university employee* make insensitive or disparaging remarks about…

|  | | Never | 1 or 2 Times | 3-5 Times | 6-9 Times | $\geq$ 10 Times |
|---|---|---|---|---|---|---|
| 1. | Men | 1 | 2 | 3 | 4 | 5 |
| 2. | Women | 1 | 2 | 3 | 4 | 5 |
| 3. | Racial/ethnic minorities | 1 | 2 | 3 | 4 | 5 |
| 4. | Gay, lesbian, bisexual persons | 1 | 2 | 3 | 4 | 5 |
| 5. | Disabled persons | 1 | 2 | 3 | 4 | 5 |
| 6. | Non-native English speakers | 1 | 2 | 3 | 4 | 5 |
| 7. | Persons of certain religious backgrounds | 1 | 2 | 3 | 4 | 5 |

C.  Since you've been at ASU, how often have you been at an *ASU event* where the persons below wouldn't have felt welcome?

|  | | Never | 1 or 2 Times | 3-5 Times | 6-9 Times | $\geq$ 10 Times |
|---|---|---|---|---|---|---|
| 1. | Men | 1 | 2 | 3 | 4 | 5 |
| 2. | Women | 1 | 2 | 3 | 4 | 5 |
| 3. | Racial/ethnic minorities | 1 | 2 | 3 | 4 | 5 |
| 4. | Gay, lesbian, bisexual persons | 1 | 2 | 3 | 4 | 5 |
| 5. | Disabled persons | 1 | 2 | 3 | 4 | 5 |
| 6. | Non-native English speakers | 1 | 2 | 3 | 4 | 5 |
| 7. | Persons of certain religious backgrounds | 1 | 2 | 3 | 4 | 5 |

D.  Have you ever felt discriminated against or harassed at ASU because you're different?

1  No  ➡  *(that ends the survey—thank you)*            2  Yes  ➡  *(Please ontinue with Item E)*

E.  I believe this discrimination or harassment was due to my…. (Check those that apply)

1. ❑  Gender
2. ❑  Age
3. ❑  Race/Ethnicity
4. ❑  Disability (Physical/Mental)

5. ❑  Sexual Orientation
6. ❑  Religious Beliefs
7. ❑  Political Beliefs
8. ❑  Other:_____

F.  What form of discrimination or harassment were you subjected to?        (Check those that apply)

1. ❑  Verbal abuse
2. ❑  Written abuse
3. ❑  Glances
4. ❑  Graffiti
5. ❑  Ignored

6. ❑  Phone calls  (other than verbal abuse)
7. ❑  Threats of physical  violence
8. ❑  Actual physical assault or injury
9. ❑  Other:_____

G.  Where did this occur?        (Check those that apply)

1. ❑  Residence Hall
2. ❑  Memorial Union
3. ❑  Walking on campus
4. ❑  ASU classroom
5. ❑  ASU office/department  _____

6. ❑  Apartment/Home
7. ❑  At work—at ASU
8. ❑  At work—not at  ASU
9. ❑  Elsewhere on or around campus

H.  Who was the source?        (Check those that apply)

1. ❑  Student(s)
2. ❑  Professor
3. ❑  Resident Advisor
4. ❑  Teaching Assistant

5. ❑  University staff/administrator
6. ❑  People in areas around campus
7. ❑  Campus police
8. ❑  Other:_____

*Thanks for your feedback and time*

# *UNI 100 Survey A*

---

In keeping with ASU s commitment to  Excellence in Undergraduate Education,  we are asking how you perceive this course, as well your expectations of ASU.  Please complete all items on this survey and respond as honestly as possible.  Responses will be confidential and will be reported only as group data.

---

**Section I**

A.  Circle one response for the item below

|  | Very Difficult | Difficult | N/A | Easy | Very Easy |
|---|---|---|---|---|---|
| 1.  I expect UNI 100 to be ........... | 1 | 2 | 3 | 4 | 5 |

B.  What do you expect to find most helpful about UNI 100?

_____

C.  Below are expectations you might have about what UNI 100 will be like or be about or help you learn.

**A.** How important is each expectation in influencing your decision to take UNI ?

| Expectation | Critical | Much | Some | Little | None |
|---|---|---|---|---|---|
| 1.  Gain a better understanding of myself | 1 | 2 | 3 | 4 | 5 |
| 2.  Develop my own set of values & ethical standards | 1 | 2 | 3 | 4 | 5 |
| 3.  Develop my study skills | 1 | 2 | 3 | 4 | 5 |
| 4.  Develop awareness of people and cultural values | 1 | 2 | 3 | 4 | 5 |
| 5.  Develop appreciation for civic & community involvement | 1 | 2 | 3 | 4 | 5 |
| 6.  Learn to withhold judgment, ask questions, & examine other views | 1 | 2 | 3 | 4 | 5 |
| 7.  Develop my test-taking skills | 1 | 2 | 3 | 4 | 5 |
| 8.  Easy grade | 1 | 2 | 3 | 4 | 5 |
| 9.  Learn about the library | 1 | 2 | 3 | 4 | 5 |
| 10.  3-hour course credit | 1 | 2 | 3 | 4 | 5 |
| 11.  Have someone I can go to if I have any questions or problems during my first semester at ASU | 1 | 2 | 3 | 4 | 5 |
| 12.  Learn about services on campus | 1 | 2 | 3 | 4 | 5 |
| 13.  Meet other students from my major with whom I can study | 1 | 2 | 3 | 4 | 5 |
| 14.  Meet other students with whom I can socialize | 1 | 2 | 3 | 4 | 5 |
| 15.  Learn what college teachers expect of me | 1 | 2 | 3 | 4 | 5 |
| 16.  Learn how to get more involved in campus activities | 1 | 2 | 3 | 4 | 5 |

D. Indicate whether you think you <u>might get involved in</u> each activity in the next six months or so.

|  |  | A. | Plan to do this | |
|---|---|---|---|---|
|  |  |  | No | Yes |
| 1. | Talk with faculty informally outside of class |  | 1 | 2 |
| 2. | Voice an opinion about a controversial issue(s) |  | 1 | 2 |
| 3. | Personally seek information which addresses issues of diversity |  | 1 | 2 |
| 4. | Become personally involved in a discussion/debate with someone whose race/ethnicity differs from your own |  | 1 | 2 |
| 5. | Participate in a student study group on your own initiative outside of class |  | 1 | 2 |
| 6. | Make friends with students whose academic/major interests differs from yours |  | 1 | 2 |
| 7. | Praise, encourage, or defend someone for his or her views on a topic |  | 1 | 2 |
| 8. | Attend an info session, talk, or meeting which addresses issues of diversity, such as race/ethnicity, women s issues, sexual orientation, etc. |  | 1 | 2 |
| 9. | Participate in serious discussions with students whose religious beliefs, life philosophies, or personal values differ from your own |  | 1 | 2 |
| 10. | Give advice, information, or assistance to someone whose race/ethnicity differs from your own |  | 1 | 2 |
| 11. | Use the library as a place to study and/or do research for classes |  | 1 | 2 |
| 12. | Seek assistance for a drug, alcohol, eating problem |  | 1 | 2 |
| 13. | Seek information on a major or career |  | 1 | 2 |

## Section II

A. How do you expect the *racial/ethnic climate* at ASU to be on the following dimensions?
(Circle one response for each)

|  |  |  |  | Neutral |  |  |  |
|---|---|---|---|---|---|---|---|
| 1. | Tense | 1 | 2 | 3 | 4 | 5 | Relaxed |
| 2. | Hostile | 1 | 2 | 3 | 4 | 5 | Friendly |
| 3. | Intolerant | 1 | 2 | 3 | 4 | 5 | Tolerant |
| 4. | Uncomfortable | 1 | 2 | 3 | 4 | 5 | Comfortable |
| 5. | Socially separated | 1 | 2 | 3 | 4 | 5 | Socially integrated |

B. How do you expect the climate at ASU to be in terms of *gender (male/female) relations*?
(Circle one response for each)

|  |  |  |  | Neutral |  |  |  |
|---|---|---|---|---|---|---|---|
| 1. | Tense | 1 | 2 | 3 | 4 | 5 | Relaxed |
| 2. | Hostile | 1 | 2 | 3 | 4 | 5 | Friendly |
| 3. | Intolerant | 1 | 2 | 3 | 4 | 5 | Tolerant |
| 4. | Uncomfortable | 1 | 2 | 3 | 4 | 5 | Comfortable |
| 5. | Socially separated | 1 | 2 | 3 | 4 | 5 | Socially integrated |

C.  How do you expect the climate at ASU to be for people of differing *sexual orientation*?
    Circle one response for each)

|    |                   | | | Neutral | | |                     |
|----|-------------------|---|---|---|---|---|---------------------|
| 1. | Tense             | 1 | 2 | 3 | 4 | 5 | Relaxed             |
| 2. | Hostile           | 1 | 2 | 3 | 4 | 5 | Friendly            |
| 3. | Intolerant        | 1 | 2 | 3 | 4 | 5 | Tolerant            |
| 4. | Uncomfortable     | 1 | 2 | 3 | 4 | 5 | Comfortable         |
| 5. | Socially separated| 1 | 2 | 3 | 4 | 5 | Socially integrated |

D.  How do you expect the climate at ASU to be for people of differing *religious groups*?
    (Circle one response for each)

|    |                   | | | Neutral | | |                     |
|----|-------------------|---|---|---|---|---|---------------------|
| 1. | Tense             | 1 | 2 | 3 | 4 | 5 | Relaxed             |
| 2. | Hostile           | 1 | 2 | 3 | 4 | 5 | Friendly            |
| 3. | Intolerant        | 1 | 2 | 3 | 4 | 5 | Tolerant            |
| 4. | Uncomfortable     | 1 | 2 | 3 | 4 | 5 | Comfortable         |
| 5. | Socially separated| 1 | 2 | 3 | 4 | 5 | Socially integrated |

**Section III.**

A.  What grade do you expect to receive in this class?

   A     B     C

*Thanks for your feedback and time.*

## Appendix B

# CURRICULUM, STUDENT LEARNING, AND FACULTY

This section contains instruments that provide ways to evaluate diversity courses. In addition, there are instruments that help determine the faculty perceptions of the educational impact of diverse students in the classroom as well as student self-reports about the quality of their education. The results can and should be disaggregated by groups.

The assessment tools* included in this appendix are:

- Assessing Diversity Courses
- AAUP/ACE Faculty Classroom Diversity Questionnaire
- Lewis and Clark Student Questionnaire
- Oberlin Student Self-Statements about Learning
- Senior Seminar Peer Interview: Oberlin College

* All assessment tools are used with permission. Please note that if you decide to use any of the assessment tools, you must obtain a separate copyright permission directly from the author/creator. The copyright holder is listed prior to each tool for your convenience.

# ASSESSING DIVERSITY COURSES

This instrument provides step-by-step instructions for assessing diversity courses. The guiding principles for assessing a diversity course are, in general, the same principles that should guide assessment of any course. This guide will help the instructor formulate and evaluate learning objectives and goals throughout the semester.

For more information contact:

Jack Meacham
Department of Psychology
323 Park Hall
SUNY at Buffalo
Buffalo, NY 14260-4110
Phone: 716-645-3650
Email: meacham@acsu.buffalo.edu

# ASSESSING DIVERSITY COURSES

## By Jack Meacham

- Articulating Learning Goals
- Assessing Before the Course Ends
- Creating Appropriate Final Course Evaluations for Diversity Classes
- Assessing Diversity Learning Goals for Students
- Assessing Classroom Atmosphere and Process
- Traditional Assessment Questions
- References

The guiding principles for assessment of a diversity course are, in general, the same principles that should guide assessment of any course. It is important to consider before the first day of class how one will know, at the end of the term, whether the goals for student learning have been met. All the efforts of the teacher and the students in a diversity course will count for little—even if the students attend regularly, complete their assignments, say that they like the course, and receive good grades—if the goals for student learning have not been met. If the course goals have not been attained, then one should want to know why not and what might be done better the next time. Even if the goals have been met successfully, it will be important in teaching the course again to know what readings or discussion topics or classroom activities were most helpful towards reaching the goals, so that these are not inadvertently dropped in a modest revision of the course.

## *Articulating Learning Goals*

Before beginning to teach a course on diversity, one should record the goals for student learning, expressing these in a form so that later assessment of student progress towards these goals is possible. At the least, this record will serve as a reminder to keep the teacher on track over several weeks of teaching, and as a point of comparison when new goals emerge as a result of interactions with students in the course. Furthermore, if the goals for student learning cannot be expressed in a measurable form, then it is likely that they have not yet been articulated sufficiently clearly in the mind of the teacher to be an adequate guide in the selection of course texts and readings, classroom activities, and discussion topics or in the evaluation of students. It is good practice to list goals for student learning on the course syllabus that is distributed to students. It clarifies the expectations for student learning in the course and serves as a reminder for both students and the teacher to stay focused on course-relevant topics in their discussions throughout the term. Goals for student learning should be limited in scope as well as appropriate for the students' learning, not the teacher's. Some of the teachers of the American Pluralism course at SUNY at Buffalo have adopted goals for student learning such as to understand ourselves and others in ways other than stereotyped groups or categories; to develop an awareness of the causes and effects of structured inequalities and prejudicial exclusion; and to develop an increased self-awareness of what it means in our culture to be a person of the student's own gender, race, class, ethnicity, and religion as well as an understanding of how these categories affect those who are different. At the most general level, many of these teachers believe that the goal of a course on diversity is for students to learn what the American experience is like for different groups of people and to understand that if they were in the situations of others they might feel similarly.

### Assessing Before the Course Ends

The usual procedure for course assessment is for a questionnaire to be administered to students towards the end of the term. Typically, however, the teacher does not receive the results until several weeks following the last class. Waiting until the end of the term to solicit feedback from students can leave the teacher uninformed about what students are really thinking in a diversity course. Most classes include both students who frequently participate in class discussions and others who sit silently or participate only infrequently. In some courses one can assume that the vocal students are representative of the viewpoints of the silent students, but this might not be the case for many contemporary, controversial issues that can arise in a diversity course. Those students who are not speaking might be in sharp disagreement with those students who are speaking, yet perhaps concerned that if they speak they will be drawn into an argument; or they might be following the discussion closely and strongly engaged and perhaps even deeply moved by what is being said; or there might be students representing both of these positions. The issues in a diversity course can touch students very personally, for dimensions such as race, gender, ethnicity, and religion are among those at the core of the identities that traditional college-age students are constructing.

It can be a mistake for a teacher in a diversity course to assume that the vocal students are representative of the opinions and feelings of the less vocal students. Instead, it is good practice to assess informally how the course is going at least once and perhaps several times as the course is progressing, especially for those who are teaching a diversity course for the first or second time, and then if necessary to make appropriate changes in readings, classroom activities, or course requirements right away. A simple assessment procedure is to bring the class to a close a few minutes early and ask the students to write anonymously what might be changed to make the class better and to leave these suggestions as they exit the classroom. Not only can good suggestions emerge, but the procedure itself reinforces an important lesson for many diversity courses, namely, that each person's opinion will be listened to and respected. Such informal yet frequent assessment and minor course corrections can make the difference between a disastrous course and one that is now back on track.

Much can be learned about how a diversity course is progressing by asking students to keep journals in which they record their brief reactions, examples, questions, disagreements, or insights in response to each assigned reading, lecture, and class discussion. Typically such journal entries are regarded as confidential, and read by no one except the teacher. Journal entries can sometimes reveal that the class as a whole has reacted to assigned readings or issues quite differently than what the teacher might otherwise assume, given what had been said aloud during class. Often teachers find that they are able to construct discussion topics and questions for future classes from some of the journal entries. Another procedure for learning about the progress of a diversity course is to provide students with the opportunity to post messages and read what their peers have to say on an electronic- mail discussion list (Meacham, 1994).

### Creating Appropriate Final Course Evaluations for Diversity Classes

The process of teaching a course on diversity should not conclude until the course itself has been evaluated against the goals for student learning that were recorded prior to teaching the course. Most standard course-evaluation questionnaires will not be adequate for the particular assessment needs of diversity courses, and so teachers must plan in advance to find or construct questionnaires that are appropriate given the particular goals they hold for student learning. One easy, yet very informative, assessment procedure is to ask students to list three aspects that they liked about the course and three things that they disliked. Another easy and informative question is to ask students to list three things that they learned in the course. If the goals for student learning are being met, then more than a few students should list information and concepts that relate to the teacher's previously recorded goals for the course. For example, a student in SUNY at Buffalo's American Pluralism course wrote at the end of the term, "There are more ways of looking at things than the one I came to class with." This comment is evidence that the student learning goal of the course, to learn about the experiences and perspectives of others, was met for this student.

### Assessing Diversity Learning Goals for Students

Often simple, ad hoc assessment questions that relate directly to the teacher's goals for the course are much more useful than the general questions that appear on standard course- evaluation questionnaires. Here are some examples of questions that could be asked at the end of the term in order to assess whether the teacher's goals for student learning have been met in the course. Of course, there are many possible goals for student learning and so there are many possible questions that could be constructed for use on an assessment questionnaire.

1. This course has helped me to understand myself and others in ways other than stereotyped groups and categories.
   A. strongly agree          B. agree          C. neutral
   D. disagree          E. strongly disagree

2. I now have an increased awareness of the causes and effects of structured inequalities and prejudicial exclusions.
   A. strongly agree          B. agree          C. neutral
   D. disagree          E. strongly disagree

3. This course has helped me to ask questions, analyze arguments, make connections, and be a better thinker.
   A. strongly agree          B. agree          C. neutral
   D. disagree          E. strongly disagree

4. This course has helped me to become more confident in stating my views and expressing myself orally.
   A. strongly agree          B. agree          C. neutral
   D. disagree          E. strongly disagree

5. As a result of taking this course, I am more likely to examine what I read closely and assess its usefulness before drawing conclusions.
   A. strongly agree          B. agree          C. neutral
   D. disagree          E. strongly disagree

6. I find myself talking with other students outside of class about the material covered in this course.
   A. strongly agree          B. agree          C. neutral
   D. disagree          E. strongly disagree

7. This course has inspired excitement in new topics, and I have considered taking additional courses related to the topics in this course.
   A. strongly agree          B. agree          C. neutral
   D. disagree          E. strongly disagree

8. This course has stimulated me to read related books and articles, and I have begun to read and listen to the news differently.

A. strongly agree      B. agree      C. neutral

D. disagree      E. strongly disagree

9. This course introduced ideas I had not previously encountered.

A. strongly agree      B. agree      C. neutral

D. disagree      E. strongly disagree

10. I have been able to see connections between the material in this course and real-life situations I might face on the job, in my family, and as a citizen.

A. strongly agree      B. agree      C. neutral

D. disagree      E. strongly disagree

11. I feel more confident about my ability to work with others as a result of this course.

A. strongly agree      B. agree      C. neutral

D. disagree      E. strongly disagree

12. I am now more convinced of the importance of the material in this course than when I began the course.

A. strongly agree      B. agree      C. neutral

D. disagree      E. strongly disagree

## Assessing Classroom Atmosphere and Process

In a course on diversity the classroom atmosphere and the interactions of the students with each other and with the teacher are critical to the success of the course. Thus it is important in assessing the course to ask questions regarding classroom atmosphere and process. Did students feel they could bring up issues in the classroom? Did students feel there was an atmosphere of respect and trust? Did the teacher allow students to express their point of view? Did the teacher respect students' opinions? These questions might appear on an assessment questionnaire in a format such as the following:

13. In this course there have been opportunities for students to bring up or discuss issues related to the course.

A. strongly agree      B. agree      C. neutral

D. disagree      E. strongly disagree

14. In this course the teacher allowed students to express their point of view and respected their opinion.

A. strongly agree      B. agree      C. neutral

D. disagree      E. strongly disagree

15. The format for this course has been primarily lecture.
    A. strongly agree          B. agree                    C. neutral
    D. disagree                E. strongly disagree

16. The format for this course has been primarily discussion, with students learning from
    each other and constructing our own understanding of the issues.
    A. strongly agree          B. agree                    C. neutral
    D. disagree                E. strongly disagree

17. In this course classroom discussions were managed so that they were a useful part of
    my learning experience.
    A. strongly agree          B. agree                    C. neutral
    D. disagree                E. strongly disagree

18. The instructor in this course asked questions that challenged me to think.
    A. strongly agree          B. agree                    C. neutral
    D. disagree                E. strongly disagree

Typically teachers receive summary data from questions such as these only after the conclusion of the course. However, a better diagnostic procedure for teachers who are new to teaching about diversity is to make assessment of the course a project for the class itself. The course goals can be shared with the students, who can then decide how to assess the course and what questions to ask. After some data have been gathered and summarized, the students can discuss the extent to which various goals were met and why, what readings or class activities were critical towards meeting those goals, and how the course might be improved for the next group of students. There is much that teachers can learn from listening to students' views and reflections on how the course progressed and what was learned and their suggestions on how the course can be strengthened.

### Traditional Assessment Questions

Next, here are a few examples of traditional assessment questions regarding materials and assignments and how much has been learned. These questions are provided here to illustrate the contrast with the earlier questions that are derived directly from the goals for student learning or that inquire about classroom atmosphere and interactions among the students and with the teacher. Of course, a few questions from each of these three categories can be mixed together in constructing a brief assessment questionnaire of half a dozen to a dozen items.

19. The workload for this course is:
    A. one of the lightest        B. lighter than average        C. about average
    D. heavier than average       E. one of the heaviest

20. The pace in this course is:
    A. too slow & sometimes boring    B. slower than average        C. about average
    D. faster than average            E. too fast for me to keep up

21. The texts and readings used in this course are:
    A. among the very best        B. better than average         C. about average
    D. worse than average         E. among the worst

22. Overall, how much do you feel you have learned in this course?
    A. an exceptional amount      B. more than usual             C. about as much as usual
    D. less than usual            E. almost nothing

23. The instructor is punctual in meeting class and office hour responsibilities.
    A. almost always              B. more than half the time     C. about half the time
    D. less than half the time    E. almost never

24. The difficulty level of the course activities and materials is:
    A. extremely easy             B. easier than average         C. about average
    D. more difficult than average    E. extremely difficult

25. What is your overall rating of the instructor's teaching effectiveness compared with
    other college instructors you have had?
    A. one of the most effective      B. more effective than average    C. about average
    D. less effective than average    E. one of the least effective

26. What is your overall rating of this course?
    A. one of the best            B. better than average         C. about average
    D. worse than average         E. one of the worst

Although the literature about assessing diversity courses is just emerging, many
practices used by student-centered assessment can easily be adapted. Two fine resources
with excellent advice about assessment procedures as well as many examples of
assessment questions are the recent books by Angelo and Cross (1993) and by Musil
(1992). The important thing to remember, however, is that every teacher has resources
for gathering immediate feedback about what students are learning in diversity courses.
That information is essential for improving what is offered to students and for increasing

our confidence that the learning goals we have articulated are being met by the course. The more we practitioners invent and share teacher- and student-friendly methods of gathering information about student learning, the more they can know about how to prepare students to be active, engaged participants in shaping the multicultural worlds they will and already do inhabit.

### References:

Angelo, T. A. & Cross, K. P. 1993. *Classroom assessment techniques: A handbook for college teachers* (2nd ed.). San Francisco: Jossey-Bass.

Meacham, J. A. 1994. Discussions by e-mail: Experiences from a large class on multiculturalism. *Liberal Education*, 80(4), 36-39.

Musil, C. M. (Ed.) 1992. *Students at the center: Feminist assessment.* Washington, D.C.: Association of American Colleges.

# ACE/AAUP
# FACULTY CLASSROOM DIVERSITY QUESTIONNAIRE

We have included the guidelines for using the Faculty Classroom Diversity Questionnaire created by the American Council on Education's (ACE) Office of Minorities in Higher Education (OMHE) and the American Association of University Professors (AAUP). The questionnaire provides information regarding faculty attitudes toward diversity. A copy of the questionnaire has not been included. Instead, we have included a copy of the guidelines, created by the authors, that must be followed and agreed upon before obtaining or using the survey.

To contact ACE's OMHE:

Linda Mabrey
American Council on Education
Office of Minorities in Higher Education
1 Dupont Circle, NW, Suite 800
Washington, DC 20036
Phone: 202-939-9395
Email: omhe@ace.nche.edu

To contact the AAUP:

Ann Springer
Associate Counsel, AAUP
1012 14th Street, NW, Suite 500
Washington, DC 20005
Phone: 202-737-5900

The original research team includes:

Jonathan R. Alger, University of Michigan
Jorge Chapa, Indiana University
Roxane Harvey Gudeman, Macalester College
Patricia Marin, The Civil Rights Project, Harvard University
Geoffrey Maruyama, University of Minnesota
Jeffrey F. Milem, University of Maryland
Jose F. Moreno, University of California, Davis
Deborah J. Wilds, Bill and Melinda Gates Foundation

## ACE/AAUP
## Faculty Classroom Diversity Questionnaire

Guidelines as of January 2001 for:
- Use of Questionnaire
- Use of Database
- Re-publishing original report

### I. Faculty Classroom Diversity Questionnaire Use:

The American Council on Education's (ACE) Office of Minorities in Higher Education (OMHE), the American Association of University Professors (AAUP), and the research team that produced the report Does Diversity Make a Difference? Three Research Studies on Diversity in College Classrooms, all continue to be interested in faculty attitudes toward diversity. Therefore, we would like to encourage others to use the Faculty Classroom Diversity Questionnaire ("the survey"), but also would like to be able to add their data to ours, expanding the database.

To encourage such use (provided users agree in writing to abide by the conditions described below):

1. ACE's OMHE will make a sample survey package available, free of charge, for use by an individual researcher or an institution. This package, all in electronic format, will include a copy of the survey as well as other materials used in the original mailing of the survey.

2. ACE's OMHE offers to provide services through the University of Minnesota's Office of Measurement Services that will help individuals/institutions that want to use the survey. The fees for these services will be the responsibility of the individual/institution using the survey. The services available are (a) making copies of the surveys on scannable forms, (b) scanning completed surveys, (c) providing basic analyses and setting up SPSS files for data analysis, (d) compiling a list of responses to open ended questions, and (e) providing analyses that parallel those reported in the ACE/AAUP monograph. For price quotes, contact Margie Tomsic at the Office of Measurement Services (OMS) of the University of Minnesota (612-525-8175; tomsic@fast.ucs.umn.edu). OMS will require proof that permission has been granted to use the survey before providing any services. We believe that because templates have already been set up by the Office of Measurement Services, these services will most likely be less expensive than those available elsewhere. However, it is not required that you use these services.

3. ACE's OMHE and AAUP will, when possible, help publicize any results from additional research using the survey (with the appropriate citation of the new work). Some examples of such assistance include citing or even summarizing the work in newsletters and adding links to the work from the ACE and/or AAUP web site.

4. ACE's OMHE, AAUP, and the original research team must grant final permission. This will be coordinated by ACE's OMHE.

Researchers/institutions wanting to use the instrument will:

1. Agree that all rights to the survey, and any derivatives thereof, remain with ACE's OMHE and AAUP.

2. Provide to ACE's OMHE a copy of the instrument that is administered, including copies of written and oral directions given when the survey was administered to respondents. If a user decides to develop a web-based version of the survey, a copy of the setup of that instrument will be provided to ACE's OMHE.

3. Provide to ACE's OMHE a data file of individual responses, stripped of any information that would uniquely identify respondents. ACE's OMHE, AAUP, and the original research team reserves the right to combine the data with data from other studies for aggregate analyses, or to conduct secondary analyses of the data. These rights are not intended to infringe upon the rights of researchers to publish their research.

4. Send ACE's OMHE copies of publications or institutional research reports that report survey results.

5. Submit all above materials within six months of the completion of their research.

Note: ACE's OMHE will be the repository of the information and data that the researcher/institution is required to submit. This will be available to the AAUP and the original research team of the faculty classroom diversity questionnaire.


## II. Database Use:

Researchers/institutions wanting to use the original national database from the Faculty Classroom Diversity Questionnaire, and/or the aggregate database, will:

1. Submit a proposal indicating the goals and objectives of the intended study, the methods to be used, the research questions that will be addressed, and the scientific and policy merit of the study.

2. ACE's OMHE, AAUP, and the original research team must grant final permission. This will be coordinated by ACE's OMHE.

### III. Re-publishing the chapters from and/or the Executive Summary of Does Diversity Make a Difference? Three Research Studies on Diversity in College Classrooms

Note: This does not refer to individual copies made for educational purposes.

1. Written requests must be submitted to ACE's OMHE.
2. In general, permission shall be limited to use for non-profit, educational purposes and the content of the work cannot be altered in any way.
3. Requests that do not meet the above criteria will be considered on a case by case basis.
4. ACE's OMHE, AAUP, (and specific author[s] if request is for individual chapter[s]) must grant final permission. This will be coordinated by ACE's OMHE.
5. The work must be listed as "reprinted with permission" and indicate the original source and author(s). The proper information to be included in the citation of the publication, executive summary, and the various chapters are as follows:

*Does Diversity Make a Difference? Three Research Studies on Diversity in College Classrooms. Executive Summary.* 2000. Washington, DC: American Council on Education and American Association of University Professors.

*Does Diversity Make a Difference? Three Research Studies on Diversity in College Classrooms.* 2000. Washington, DC: American Council on Education and American Association of University Professors.

Maruyama, G., & Moreno, J. F. 2000. University faculty views about the value of diversity on campus and in the classroom. In *Does Diversity Make a Difference? Three Research Studies on Diversity in College Classrooms* (pp. 9-35). Washington, DC: American Council on Education and American Association of University Professors.

Gudeman, R. H. 2000. College missions, faculty teaching, and student outcomes in a context of low diversity. In *Does Diversity Make a Difference? Three Research Studies on Diversity in College Classrooms* (pp. 37-60). Washington, DC: American Council on Education and American Association of University Professors.

Marin, P. 2000. The educational possibility of multi-racial/multi-ethnic college classrooms. In *Does Diversity Make a Difference? Three Research Studies on Diversity in College Classrooms* (pp. 61-83). Washington, DC: American Council on Education and American Association of University Professors.

# STUDENT QUESTIONNAIRE
# LEWIS AND CLARK COLLEGE

This instrument will help to assess how effectively students learn and apply gender analysis as well as the impact gender studies has had on the classroom and institutional climates at Lewis and Clark. This questionnaire provides data about Lewis and Clark's Gender Studies program, including student learning, integration efforts, and personal growth.

This questionnaire was part of a three-year women's studies assessment project funded by the US Department of Education's Fund for the Improvement of Postsecondary Education (FIPSE). The results are published in AAC&U's *The Courage to Question: Women's Studies and Student Learning* (1990) and *Students at the Center* (1992).

For more information:

Jean M. Ward
Professor of Communication/Director of Inventing America
Communication, Campus Box 35
0615 S.W. Palatine Hill Road
Portland, Oregon 97219-7899
Phone: 503-768-7613
Email: jean@lclark.edu

# STUDENT QUESTIONNAIRE
# LEWIS AND CLARK COLLEGE

Male:

Female:

Age:

Year in School:

Major:

Minor:

## Part I: Gender Studies Program

1. What do you think are the objectives of the Gender Studies Program at Lewis and Clark?

2. How well do you believe these objectives are being met? (What particular strengths and weaknesses do you perceive?)

3. What difference, if any, do you see between a gender studies program and a women's studies program?

4. What impact, if any, do you believe the gender studies program has had on Lewis and Clark?

5. In your opinion, should Lewis and Clark have a gender studies program? Why or why not?

## Part II: Gender Studies Core Courses

1. Indicate which, if any, of the following gender studies core courses you have completed and in which courses you are currently enrolled:

   C = completed course, E = enrolled course

   [List of courses followed on original questionnaire]

2. Circle the number on the scale that best represents your overall learning in the above gender studies core courses:

| 1 | 2 | 3 | 4 | 5 |
|---|---|---|---|---|
| poor | fair | average | good | excellent |

3. What do you consider to be your most significant and least significant learning experiences in these courses?

4. How do these gender studies core courses compare with other courses you have taken at Lewis and Clark?

5. Was the learning/teaching climate in these gender studies core courses different from your non-gender studies classes? If so, how?

6. What effect, if any, have these gender studies core courses had on your understanding of issues of gender, race, and class?

7. Which of these courses would you recommend to other students? Why?

## Part III: Practicum/Internship in Gender Studies

If you completed or are currently involved in a practicum/internship in gender studies, describe the practicum and comment on the experience:

## Part IV: Other Courses with a Gender Focus

1. What other courses have you taken in the Lewis and Clark general college curriculum that included a focus on gender issues?

2. Circle the number on the scale that best represents your overall learning in these courses:

| 1 | 2 | 3 | 4 | 5 |
|---|---|---|---|---|
| poor | fair | average | good | excellent |

3. What do you consider to be your most significant and least significant learning experience in these courses?

4. How do these courses compare with other courses you have taken at Lewis and Clark?

5. Which of these courses would your recommend to other students? Why?

## Part V: Gender and Overseas Programs

1. Have you participated in a Lewis and Clark overseas program?     Yes     No
   If yes, what was the program?

2. How did gender issues figure in the program—in preparation, during the course of the overseas study, after return to campus?

### Part VI: Gender Studies Symposium

1. Have you ever attended any of the Lewis and Clark Gender Studies Symposium events?    Yes    No

If yes, circle the year(s) of your participation in the symposium?

1982      1983      1984      1985      1986      1987      1988      1989      1990

2. Which events do you recall attending, and what was your evaluation?

3. What effect did your attendance at the symposium have on your understanding of issues of gender, race, and class?

4. Circle the number of the scale that best represents your learning experience in the symposium?

| 1 | 2 | 3 | 4 | 5 |
|---|---|---|---|---|
| poor | fair | average | good | excellent |

5. Have you ever been involved as a planner, presenter, or moderator in a Lewis and Clark Gender Studies Symposium?    Yes        No

If yes, circle the year(s) of your participation in the symposium?

1982      1983      1984      1985      1986      1987      1988      1989      1990

6. Describe and comment on your participation in the symposium:

7. What effect did your participation in the symposium have on your understanding of issues of gender, race, and class?

8. Circle the number of the scale that best represents your learning experience as a symposium planner, presenter, and/or moderator:

| 1 | 2 | 3 | 4 | 5 |
|---|---|---|---|---|
| poor | fair | average | good | excellent |

# OBERLIN STUDENT SELF-STATEMENTS ABOUT LEARNING AND SENIOR SEMINAR PEER INTERVIEW

These instruments seek to answer the following questions: What fosters student learning and self-empowerment? How can courses encourage a relational understanding of gender, race, class, and sexuality? Does feminist pedagogy differ from other types? How do women's studies courses affect students' lives and life choices? A set of student interviews conducted by a senior women's studies major have been included to provide varying perspectives. These questionnaires were part of a three-year women's studies assessment project funded by the US Department of Education's Fund for the Improvement of Postsecondary Education (FIPSE). The results are published in AAC&U's *The Courage to Question: Women's Studies and Student Learning (1990) and Students at the Center* (1992).

For more information about these questionnaires or the project contact:
Dr. Caryn McTighe Musil
Vice-President, Diversity, Equity, and Global Initiatives
Association of American Colleges and Universities
1818 R Street, NW
Washington, DC  20009
Phone:  202-387-3760
Email:  musil@aacu.nw.dc.us

OUACHITA TECHNICAL COLLEGE

# OBERLIN STUDENT SELF STATEMENTS
# ABOUT LEARNING

### Student Self Statement #1

1. Do you expect this class to address questions of race?

   Do you expect this class to address questions of gender?

   Do you expect this class to address questions of sexuality?

   Do you expect this class to address questions of social class?

2. Do you expect this class to take a feminist approach? What does this mean for you? For example, does it mean:

   a. inclusion of women authors, artists, scientists, etc., in the syllabus

   b. discussion of systems of race, gender, and class

   c. an analysis of power relations in terms of hierarchy, oppression, and exploration

   d. other:

3. What kind of learning environment do you expect? For example, only lecture, only discussion, both lectures and discussion, student-led discussion, faculty led discussion? Other?

4. What kind of learning environment do you prefer or learn best in?

5. If you expect discussion, do you expect to be actively engaged in discussion or do you expect the teacher to lead most of the discussion?

6. What do you hope to learn in this class?

### Student Self-Statement #2

1. Does this class address questions of race? How?

   Does this class address questions of gender? How?

   Does this class address questions of sexuality? How?

   Does this class address questions of social class? How?

2. Is this class taking a feminist approach? Please explain.

3. Collaborative learning is defined as a pedagogical style that emphasizes cooperative efforts among students and faculty members. It is rooted in the belief that learning is social in nature and stresses common inquiry as a basic learning process. Do you think collaborative learning has taken place in your classroom? In what specific ways?

4. Since true collaborative learning means working with and learning from people who are different from oneself, how have you negotiated and mediated those differences?

5. What are some of the significant things you are learning in this class?

### Student Self Statement #3

1. Has this class addressed questions of race?  How?
   Has this class addressed questions of gender?  How?
   Has this class addressed questions of sexuality?  How?
   Has this class addressed questions of social class?  How?

2. How would you characterize the most important things you have learned in this class (in terms of context and process)?

# SENIOR SEMINAR PEER INTERVIEW
# OBERLIN COLLEGE

## *Instructions*

1. Please audiotape the entire interview, and turn in the cassettes with your summary of the interview.
2. I expect you to spend about 45 minutes on each interview.
3. Be sure you ask the questions listed below, but feel free to add questions. While this will help the Program with the NWSA/FIPSE Assessment Project, I also want you to be able to make sense of our WOST experience for yourselves.
4. Write up a five-page report, summarizing the responses of the person your inter-view. Do not transcribe the tape but use direct quotes in your summary. Organize the summary in terms of the questions below, or in terms of categories as they emerge from your conversation/interview.

## *Peer Interview Questions*

1. How did you become a WOST major?

2. Summarize what you consider to be your most important "learning" as a WOST major. What did you take from WOST to other classes?

3. Can you identify one or two significant experiences at Oberlin (a course, an event, a professor, friendships, membership in political organizations, etc.) that most influenced your feminist consciousness?

4. Briefly describe changes in your expectations of the content and process of your WOST education from the time you were a freshperson through your senior year.

5. How has WOST affected your intellectual life, your political beliefs, and your personal life? Please describe any other significant changes.

6. Goals of the Oberlin WOST Program include self empowerment; recognition of differences; collaborative learning; understanding interdisciplinary connection in the analysis of gender, race, class, and sexuality; and linking personal with social responsibility. Which of these goals are most important to you and which do you feel you have accomplished as a student in WOST?

7. Which of the following activities do you consider most important for the future of WOST at Oberlin. Please rank in order of importance (1 = most important):

____Change status from program to department.

____ Increase number of full-time faculty members in WOST.

____ Increase visibility of program within and outside the college.

____ Raise funds from alumni/ae to create endowed chair in WOST.

____ Improve representation of women of color on faculty, among students and staff, and in the curriculum.

____ Lobby administration and trustees for more support for program.

8. What kinds of things (jobs, further education, communities) are you looking for after graduation? How does being a WOST student influence your quest?

9. Is there anything else you want to add about what it has meant to be a WOST major at Oberlin? Can you identify gaps in your experience as a major? What needs improvement?

# Appendix C

# INSTITUTIONAL OVERVIEWS

The instruments contained in this section represent broader ways to gather more comprehensive campus profiles and means to probe constituents not yet examined. This section includes a student and alumni questionnaire as well as an index of the institution's overall commitment to multiculturalism.

The assessment tools* included in this appendix are:

- University of Washington's Campus Climate Survey for Current Students and Alumni
- Hale Inventory of Commitment to Multiculturalism

* All assessment tools are used with permission. Please note that if you decide to use any of the assessment tools, you must obtain a separate copyright permission directly from the author/creator. The copyright holder is listed prior to each tool for your convenience.

# CAMPUS CLIMATE SURVEY:
## CURRENT STUDENTS AND ALUMNI

## UNIVERSITY OF WASHINGTON

The first instrument measures the relationships among current students' perceptions of campus climate and their academic achievement. It is comprised of several sections assessing various aspects of campus climate as well as selected demographic characteristics and other possible correlates. The second instrument, a modification of the first, is designed for University of Washington alumni with specific questions about the work climate and diversity.

For more information contact:

Nana Lowell
Associate Director
Office of Educational Assessment
University of Washington
Seattle, WA 98195-5837
Phone: 206-543-9956
Email: nlowell@u.washington.edu

# I. CURRENT STUDENTS

### University of Washington

# Campus Climate Survey

*Use a No. 2 pencil*
*Fill bubbles darkly and completely.*
*Do not make stray marks.*
*Erase completely.*

**CURRENT STUDENTS**

**SECTION A.** The following questions ask for information about you and your present situation. Remember, *all information that you provide is anonymous and will be reported only in combination with other responses*.

1. Your academic class?

    Junior
    Senior

2. Your gender?

    Male
    Female

5. Your academic major/program?

_____

3. Which one of following racial / ethnic groups *best* describes you?

    Black or African American
    Asian American/Pacific Islander
    Hispanic or Latino
    Native American/American Indian
    White or European American
    Combination (specify):
    Other (specify):

    _____

6. Are you active in any campus clubs or other groups?

    No

    Yes ( specify):

    _____

4. Your age?

| ① | ① |
|---|---|
| ② | ② |
| ③ | ③ |
| ④ | ④ |
| ⑤ | ⑤ |
| ⑥ | ⑥ |
| ⑦ | ⑦ |
| ⑧ | ⑧ |
| ⑨ | ⑨ |

**SECTION B.** *How much do you agree or disagree* with each of the following statements? There are no right or wrong answers, just select the answer that best reflects your own feelings and beliefs.

| | DISAGREE | | | AGREE | | |
|---|---|---|---|---|---|---|
| | Strongly | Moderately | Slightly | Slightly | Moderately | Strongly |
| 1. Overall, my educational experience at the UW has been a rewarding one. | ① | ② | ③ | ④ | ⑤ | ⑥ |
| 2. I would recommend the UW to a sibling or friend as a good place to go to college. | ① | ② | ③ | ④ | ⑤ | ⑥ |
| 3. The overall quality of academic programs at the UW is excellent. | ① | ② | ③ | ④ | ⑤ | ⑥ |
| 4. The UW provides an environment for the free and open expression of ideas, opinions and beliefs. | ① | ② | ③ | ④ | ⑤ | ⑥ |
| 5. I am confident that I made the right decision in choosing to attend the UW. | ① | ② | ③ | ④ | ⑤ | ⑥ |
| 6. I feel as though I belong in the UW community. | ① | ② | ③ | ④ | ⑤ | ⑥ |
| 7. Faculty treat me fairly. | ① | ② | ③ | ④ | ⑤ | ⑥ |
| 8. Teaching assistants treat me fairly. | ① | ② | ③ | ④ | ⑤ | ⑥ |
| 9. Other students treat me fairly. | ① | ② | ③ | ④ | ⑤ | ⑥ |
| 10. The courses I enjoy the most are those that make me think about things from a different perspective. | ① | ② | ③ | ④ | ⑤ | ⑥ |
| 11. I enjoy taking courses that challenge my beliefs and values. | ① | ② | ③ | ④ | ⑤ | ⑥ |
| 12. Learning about people from different cultures is a very important part of college education. | ① | ② | ③ | ④ | ⑤ | ⑥ |
| 13. The real value of college education lies in being introduced to different values. | ① | ② | ③ | ④ | ⑤ | ⑥ |
| 14. I enjoy talking with people who have values different from mine because it helps me understand myself and my values better. | ① | ② | ③ | ④ | ⑤ | ⑥ |
| 15. Courses I enjoy most emphasize traditional values and perspectives. | ① | ② | ③ | ④ | ⑤ | ⑥ |
| 16. Contact with individuals who are different from me (e.g., race, national origin, sex, and sexual orientation) are an essential part of my college education. | ① | ② | ③ | ④ | ⑤ | ⑥ |

**SECTION C.** *How much do you agree or disagree* with each of the following statements? There are no right or wrong answers, just select the answer that best reflects your own feelings and beliefs.

| | DISAGREE | | | AGREE | | |
|---|---|---|---|---|---|---|
| | Strongly | Moderately | Slightly | Slightly | Moderately | Strongly |
| 1. If I work hard I am almost always assured of getting the grade I want to achieve. | ① | ② | ③ | ④ | ⑤ | ⑥ |
| 2. I have been exposed to racial / ethnic conflict on campus. | ① | ② | ③ | ④ | ⑤ | ⑥ |
| 3. I am often ignored in class even when I attempt to participate. | ① | ② | ③ | ④ | ⑤ | ⑥ |
| 4. When I make a comment in the classroom I am usually taken seriously by the instructor. | ① | ② | ③ | ④ | ⑤ | ⑥ |
| 5. When we work in small groups in class, I usually emerge as a leader. | ① | ② | ③ | ④ | ⑤ | ⑥ |
| 6. When we work in small groups in class, I am often ignored by my classmates or given trivial jobs. | ① | ② | ③ | ④ | ⑤ | ⑥ |
| 7. Faculty members recognize that I have important ideas to contribute. | ① | ② | ③ | ④ | ⑤ | ⑥ |
| 8. Sometimes I get singled out in class to speak on behalf of a specific racial / ethnic perspective. | ① | ② | ③ | ④ | ⑤ | ⑥ |
| 9. Sometimes faculty make inappropriate jokes about people who are different. | ① | ② | ③ | ④ | ⑤ | ⑥ |
| 10. Faculty members respect me as a person. | ① | ② | ③ | ④ | ⑤ | ⑥ |
| 11. I have been the brunt of stereotypes in the classroom. | ① | ② | ③ | ④ | ⑤ | ⑥ |
| 12. I feel isolated on campus. | ① | ② | ③ | ④ | ⑤ | ⑥ |
| 13. I have been exposed to a racist atmosphere in the classroom. | ① | ② | ③ | ④ | ⑤ | ⑥ |
| 14. I have been exposed to a racist atmosphere outside of the classroom. | ① | ② | ③ | ④ | ⑤ | ⑥ |
| 15. Most professors communicate that I am welcome in their classroom. | ① | ② | ③ | ④ | ⑤ | ⑥ |

**SECTION D.** *How have you changed* because of your experiences at UW? Remember, there are no right or wrong answers, just select the answer that best reflects your own feelings and beliefs.

| | DISAGREE | | | AGREE | | |
|---|---|---|---|---|---|---|
| | Strongly | Moderately | Slightly | Slightly | Moderately | Strongly |
| 1. I am more likely to discuss topics related to cultural diversity with friends. | ① | ② | ③ | ④ | ⑤ | ⑥ |
| 2. I am more likely to stop myself from using language that may be offensive to others. | ① | ② | ③ | ④ | ⑤ | ⑥ |
| 3. I am better able to handle negative language used by another in such a way as to try to educate the other person. | ① | ② | ③ | ④ | ⑤ | ⑥ |
| 4. I am more likely to initiate contact with people who are not of my culture or racial / ethnic background. | ① | ② | ③ | ④ | ⑤ | ⑥ |
| 5. I have a greater understanding of racial / ethnic differences. | ① | ② | ③ | ④ | ⑤ | ⑥ |
| 6. I have a greater understanding of diversity in general. | | | | | | |

**SECTION E.** *How helpful* have each of the following UW services been to you?

| | Never Used | Not at all Helpful | Not very Helpful | So-So | Somewhat Helpful | Extremely Helpful |
|---|---|---|---|---|---|---|
| 1. Academic Advising | 0 | ① | ② | ③ | ④ | ⑤ |
| 2. Career Services | 0 | ① | ② | ③ | ④ | ⑤ |
| 3. Counseling Center | | | | | | |
| 4. Department Advisor | 0 | ① | ② | ③ | ④ | ⑤ |
| 5. EOP Counselor | 0 | ① | ② | ③ | ④ | ⑤ |
| 6. Ethnic Cultural Center | 0 | ① | ② | ③ | ④ | ⑤ |
| 7. Financial Aid Office | 0 | ① | ② | ③ | ④ | ⑤ |
| 8. Hall Health Center | 0 | ① | ② | ③ | ④ | ⑤ |
| 9. Housing Services | 0 | ① | ② | ③ | ④ | ⑤ |
| 10. Student Activities Office | 0 | ① | ② | ③ | ④ | ⑤ |
| 11. Study Skills Center | 0 | ① | ② | ③ | ④ | ⑤ |
| 12. Office of Minority Affairs | 0 | ① | ② | ③ | ④ | ⑤ |

**SECTION F.**  We would like to learn about specific racial / ethnic incidents at the UW and how they were handled.  Have you observed or personally experienced such an incident?

   No, I have not observed or personally experienced any racial / ethnic incident at the UW.

   Yes, I have observed or personally experienced <u>one</u> such incident at the UW.

   Yes, I have observed or personally experienced <u>two to five</u> such incidents at the UW.

   Yes, I have observed or personally experienced <u>six to ten</u> such incidents at the UW.

   Yes, I have observed or personally experienced <u>more than ten</u> such incidents at the UW.  (Estimate total number:  _____.)

If you answered 'Yes,' was it a     negative,     neutral, or     positive incident?  Please tell us about it.  If you can think of more than one, tell us about the incident that had the greatest impact on you.

Describe what happened:




Did you report the incident to someone?        Yes        No     If yes, to whom did you report it?  _____

What, if anything, happened after the incident itself?  _____

**ADDITIONAL COMMENTS:**

## II. ALUMNI

**University of Washington**

# Campus Climate Survey

*Use a No. 2 pencil*
*Fill bubbles darkly and completely*
*Do not make stray marks.*
*Erase completely.*

ALUMNI

**SECTION A.** The following questions ask for information about you and your present situation. Remember, *all information that you provide is anonymous and will be reported only in combination with other responses*.

1. In which year did you receive your baccalaureate degree from the UW?

   1998
   1996
   1994

2. Your academic major at the UW?

   _____

3. Which one of following racial / ethnic groups **best** describes you?

   Black or African American
   Asian American/Pacific Islander
   Hispanic or Latino
   Native American/American Indian
   White or European American
   Combination (specify):
   Other (specify):

   _____

4. Your age?

| ι | ι |
|---|---|
| ① | ① |
| ② | ② |
| ③ | ③ |
| ④ | ④ |
| ⑤ | ⑤ |
| ⑥ | ⑥ |
| ⑦ | ⑦ |
| ⑧ | ⑧ |
| ⑨ | ⑨ |

5. Your gender?

   Male
   Female

6. What is your **current primary activity** (choose one)?

   Work            Looking for work
   School
   Other (specify): _____

**SECTION B.** *How much do you agree or disagree* with each of the following statements? There are no right or wrong answers, just select the answer that best reflects your own feelings and beliefs.

| | DISAGREE | | | AGREE | | |
|---|---|---|---|---|---|---|
| | Strongly | Moderately | Slightly | Slightly | Moderately | Strongly |
| 1. Overall, my educational experience at the UW was a rewarding one. | ① | ② | ③ | ④ | ⑤ | ⑥ |
| 2. I would recommend the UW to a sibling or friend as a good place to go to college. | ① | ② | ③ | ④ | ⑤ | ⑥ |
| 3. The overall quality of academic programs at the UW is excellent. | ① | ② | ③ | ④ | ⑤ | ⑥ |
| 4. The UW provides an environment for the free and open expression of ideas, opinions and beliefs. | ① | ② | ③ | ④ | ⑤ | ⑥ |
| 5. I am confident that I made the right decision in choosing to attend the UW. | ① | ② | ③ | ④ | ⑤ | ⑥ |
| 6. When I was at the UW, I felt as though I belonged in the UW community. | ① | ② | ③ | ④ | ⑤ | ⑥ |
| 7. Faculty treated me fairly. | ① | ② | ③ | ④ | ⑤ | ⑥ |
| 8. Teaching assistants treated me fairly. | ① | ② | ③ | ④ | ⑤ | ⑥ |
| 9. Other students treated me fairly. | ① | ② | ③ | ④ | ⑤ | ⑥ |
| 10. The courses I enjoyed the most were those that made me think about things from a different perspective. | ① | ② | ③ | ④ | ⑤ | ⑥ |
| 11. I enjoyed taking courses that challenged my beliefs and values. | ① | ② | ③ | ④ | ⑤ | ⑥ |
| 12. Learning about people from different cultures is a very important part of college education. | ① | ② | ③ | ④ | ⑤ | ⑥ |
| 13. A real value of college education lies in being introduced to different values. | ① | ② | ③ | ④ | ⑤ | ⑥ |
| 14. I enjoy talking with people who have values different from mine because it helps me understand myself and my values better. | ① | ② | ③ | ④ | ⑤ | ⑥ |
| 15. Courses I enjoyed most emphasized traditional values and perspectives. | ① | ② | ③ | ④ | ⑤ | ⑥ |
| 16. Contact with individuals who are different from me (e.g., race, national origin, sex, and sexual orientation) was an essential part of my college education. | ① | ② | ③ | ④ | ⑤ | ⑥ |

**SECTION C.** *How much do you agree or disagree* with each of the following statements? There are no right or wrong answers, just select the answer that best reflects your own feelings and beliefs.

| When I was at the UW: | DISAGREE | | | AGREE | | |
|---|---|---|---|---|---|---|
| | Strongly | Moderately | Slightly | Slightly | Moderately | Strongly |
| 1. If I worked hard I was almost always assured of getting the grade I wanted to achieve. | ① | ② | ③ | ④ | ⑤ | ⑥ |
| 2. I was exposed to racial / ethnic conflict on campus. | ① | ② | ③ | ④ | ⑤ | ⑥ |
| 3. I was often ignored in class even when I attempted to participate. | ① | ② | ③ | ④ | ⑤ | ⑥ |
| 4. When I made a comment in the classroom I was usually taken seriously by the instructor. | ① | ② | ③ | ④ | ⑤ | ⑥ |
| 5. When we worked in small groups in class, I usually emerged as a leader. | ① | ② | ③ | ④ | ⑤ | ⑥ |
| 6. When we worked in small groups in class, I was often ignored by my classmates or given trivial jobs. | ① | ② | ③ | ④ | ⑤ | ⑥ |
| 7. Faculty members recognized that I had important ideas to contribute. | ① | ② | ③ | ④ | ⑤ | ⑥ |
| 8. Sometimes I got singled out in class to speak on behalf of a specific racial / ethnic perspective. | ① | ② | ③ | ④ | ⑤ | ⑥ |
| 9. Sometimes faculty made inappropriate jokes about people who were different. | ① | ② | ③ | ④ | ⑤ | ⑥ |
| 10. Faculty members respected me as a person. | ① | ② | ③ | ④ | ⑤ | ⑥ |
| 11. I was the brunt of stereotypes in class. | ① | ② | ③ | ④ | ⑤ | ⑥ |
| 12. I felt isolated on campus. | ① | ② | ③ | ④ | ⑤ | ⑥ |
| 13. I was exposed to a racist atmosphere in the classroom. | ① | ② | ③ | ④ | ⑤ | ⑥ |
| 14. I was exposed to a racist atmosphere outside of the classroom. | ① | ② | ③ | ④ | ⑤ | ⑥ |
| 15. Most professors communicated that I am welcome in their classroom. | ① | ② | ③ | ④ | ⑤ | ⑥ |

**We wish to compare your experiences at the UW with those since you have graduated.**
**\* PLEASE ANSWER QUESTIONS IN THIS SECTION ONLY IF YOU ARE CURRENTLY EMPLOYED. \***

**SECTION D.** *How much do you agree or disagree* with each of the following statements? There are no right or wrong answers, just select the answer that best reflects your own feelings and beliefs.

| In my current job: | DISAGREE | | | AGREE | | |
|---|---|---|---|---|---|---|
| | Strongly | Moderately | Slightly | Slightly | Moderately | Strongly |
| 1. If I work hard I am almost always assured of being rewarded. | ① | ② | ③ | ④ | ⑤ | ⑥ |
| 2. I have been exposed to racial / ethnic conflict at work. | ① | ② | ③ | ④ | ⑤ | ⑥ |
| 3. I am often ignored at work even when I attempt to participate. | ① | ② | ③ | ④ | ⑤ | ⑥ |
| 4. When I make a comment at work I am usually taken seriously by my supervisor. | ① | ② | ③ | ④ | ⑤ | ⑥ |
| 5. When we work in small groups, I usually emerge as a leader. | ① | ② | ③ | ④ | ⑤ | ⑥ |
| 6. When we work in small groups, I am often ignored by my co-workers or given trivial jobs. | ① | ② | ③ | ④ | ⑤ | ⑥ |
| 7. Supervisors recognize that I have important ideas to contribute. | ① | ② | ③ | ④ | ⑤ | ⑥ |
| 8. Sometimes I get singled out at work to speak on behalf of a specific racial / ethnic perspective. | ① | ② | ③ | ④ | ⑤ | ⑥ |
| 9. Sometimes supervisors make inappropriate jokes about people who are different. | ① | ② | ③ | ④ | ⑤ | ⑥ |
| 10. Supervisors respect me as a person. | ① | ② | ③ | ④ | ⑤ | ⑥ |
| 11. I have been the brunt of stereotypes at work. | ① | ② | ③ | ④ | ⑤ | ⑥ |
| 12. I feel isolated at work. | ① | ② | ③ | ④ | ⑤ | ⑥ |
| 13. I have been exposed to a racist atmosphere at work. | ① | ② | ③ | ④ | ⑤ | ⑥ |

**SECTION E.** We would like to learn about specific racial / ethnic incidents at the UW and how they were handled. Did you observe or personally experience such an incident?

No, I did not observe or personally experience any racial / ethnic incident at the UW.

Yes, I observed or personally experienced <u>one</u> such incident at the UW.

Yes, I observed or personally experienced <u>two to five</u> such incidents at the UW.

Yes, I observed or personally experienced <u>six to ten</u> such incidents at the UW.

Yes, I observed or personally experienced <u>more than ten</u> such incidents at the UW. (Estimate total number: _____.)

If you answered 'Yes,' was it a     negative,     neutral, or     positive incident?  Please tell us about it.  If you can think of more than one, tell us about the incident that had the greatest impact on you.

Describe what happened:

Did you report the incident to someone?          Yes          No      If yes, to whom did you report it?      _____

What, if anything, happened after the incident itself?

**ADDITIONAL COMMENTS:**

# HALE INVENTORY OF COMMITMENT
# TO MULTICULTURALISM

The Hale Inventory, which measures attitudes and behaviors, is designed to assess an institution's commitment to multiculturalism. This inventory can assist campus personnel and offices evaluate various aspects of the institution to determine their effectiveness in providing a dynamic pluralistic environment on campus. The instrument is copyrighted and can be purchased from Frank Hale, Columbus, Ohio.

For more information contact:

Frank Hale
Vice Provost & Professor Emeritus
Distinguished University Representative/Consultant
Ohio State University
501 Fawcett Center
2400 Olentangy Road
Columbus, OH 43210
Phone: 614-688-4255

# HALE INVENTORY OF COMMITMENT TO MULTICULTURALISM

## INTRODUCTION

There is documented evidence that improving educational opportunities for students, faculty, and personnel of color in higher education achieves improved educational results. In an attempt to fill the great gaps that exist between most Americans of color and white Americans, a number of institutions of higher education are making efforts to remove the barriers that have made it difficult for students, faculty, and staff of color to have access to and experience the high-quality education available to other campus constituents.

The purpose of this inventory is to assist institutional personnel and units (faculty, administrators, departments, colleges, and universities), to evaluate various aspects of the institution (traditions, policies, practices, goals), and to determine their effectiveness in providing a dynamic pluralistic environment on their campuses. The inventory is divided into eight areas: Administrative Leadership, Admissions and Recruitment, Financial Assistance, Student Support Services, Curriculum, Campus Environment, Graduate and Professional Programs, and Multicultural Hiring.

The inventory should be useful in promoting discussions on how best an institution can develop and implement strategies to facilitate multicultural programming and affirmative action throughout the fabric of the organization as well as within individual units.

## SUMMARY

This inventory spans a comprehensive schematic for assessing, implementing, and improving the environment for diversity on a college or university campus. The assessment may be done by administrators, faculty, or students. All three approaches could be helpful in obtaining a comprehensive view of how the campus community feels about the institution's commitment to diversity.

While administrators and faculty are key figures in promoting a positive climate for diversity, students and staff bear no small share of responsibility in creating a climate that fosters a commitment to equal opportunity and social justice. Some positive initiatives that have been documented and should be encouraged are:

- Formulating a forthright vision and commitment to diversity by the president and his/her administrative staff;

- Developing a team of deans, departmental chairs, faculty, staff and student leaders who are jointly committed to achieving diversity;
- Creating a climate for discussion, dialogue, and debate on issues of diversity;
- Setting admission criteria that include factors other than quantitative ones for admissibility;
- Providing priority consideration and financial support that traditionally has been underfunded;
- Placing a high value on establishing retention strategies that will enable members of underrepresented groups to persist and graduate;
- Recognizing the unique experiences and contributions of people of color by establishing the principles of justice and multiculturalism to be reflected in the institution's curricula and its invitation of scholars and artists of color to participate in campus events;
- Encouraging the social bonding of students from a common culture in affirming their right to be drawn to each other and to have some campus space set aside where they can engage in social and educational exchanges;
- Developing strategies to identify capable undergraduates as prospective graduate students, so as to provide them with funding support and mentoring opportunities that will ensure their success as students and as future family members;
- Hiring faculty of color and establishing mentoring programs for junior faculty to facilitate their requirements for promotion and tenure.

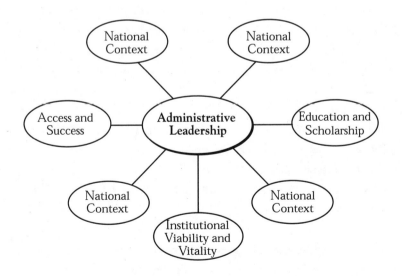

## I. INSTITUTIONAL COMMITMENT BEGINS WITH ADMINISTRATIVE LEADERSHIP

1. The administration makes serious efforts to develop and implement policies to increase the representation of people of color.

| Very | Often | Occasionally | Rarely | Never |
|------|-------|--------------|--------|-------|
| ❑ | ❑ | ❑ | ❑ | ❑ |

2. The campus community is apprised of the short- and long-range goals designed to promote cultural diversity.

| Very | Often | Occasionally | Rarely | Never |
|------|-------|--------------|--------|-------|
| ❑ | ❑ | ❑ | ❑ | ❑ |

3. The level of multicultural programming is prominent within each unit throughout the institution.

| Very | Often | Occasionally | Rarely | Never |
|------|-------|--------------|--------|-------|
| ❑ | ❑ | ❑ | ❑ | ❑ |

4. A cumulative record of information on faculty and staff of color is collected and distributed throughout the institution annually.

| Very | Often | Occasionally | Rarely | Never |
|------|-------|--------------|--------|-------|
| ❑ | ❑ | ❑ | ❑ | ❑ |

5. Staff development seminars and workshops are conducted to acquaint institutional personnel with the goals and procedures for creating a more diverse community on campus.

| Very | Often | Occasionally | Rarely | Never |
|------|-------|--------------|--------|-------|
| ❑ | ❑ | ❑ | ❑ | ❑ |

6. Special linkages are developed between the institution and local community (schools, parents, churches, and organizations) to promote early planning for children to attend college.

| Very | Often | Occasionally | Rarely | Never |
|------|-------|--------------|--------|-------|
| ❑ | ❑ | ❑ | ❑ | ❑ |

7. Articulation agreements are developed to promote and encourage the transfer of students of color from community colleges to the institution.

| Very | Often | Occasionally | Rarely | Never |
|------|-------|--------------|--------|-------|
| ❑ | ❑ | ❑ | ❑ | ❑ |

8. The institution provides special incentives and rewards to personnel and units for being effective in making ethnic cultural diversity a high priority.

| Very | Often | Occasionally | Rarely | Never |
|------|-------|--------------|--------|-------|
| ❑ | ❑ | ❑ | ❑ | ❑ |

9. Multicultural programming is supported, for the most part, by institutional monies.

| Very | Often | Occasionally | Rarely | Never |
|------|-------|--------------|--------|-------|
| ❑ | ❑ | ❑ | ❑ | ❑ |

10. The institution develops and enforces policies against discrimination, racial harassment, and "stonewalling."

| Very | Often | Occasionally | Rarely | Never |
|------|-------|--------------|--------|-------|
| ❑ | ❑ | ❑ | ❑ | ❑ |

Comments_____

## II. ADMISSIONS AND RECRUITMENT

1. The institution offers an optional 13th-year program.

| Very | Often | Occasionally | Rarely | Never |
|------|-------|--------------|--------|-------|
| ❑ | ❑ | ❑ | ❑ | ❑ |

2. Institutional programs are targeted involving high school counselors in the recruitment of students of color.

| Very | Often | Occasionally | Rarely | Never |
|------|-------|--------------|--------|-------|
| ❑ | ❑ | ❑ | ❑ | ❑ |

3. A systematic effort is underway to involve institutional alumni in the recruitment of students of color.

| Very | Often | Occasionally | Rarely | Never |
|------|-------|--------------|--------|-------|
| ❑ | ❑ | ❑ | ❑ | ❑ |

4. Offices are set up at high school sites to ensure that these students are aware of college entrance requirements.

| Very | Often | Occasionally | Rarely | Never |
|------|-------|--------------|--------|-------|
| ❑ | ❑ | ❑ | ❑ | ❑ |

5. The cooperation of the media (radio, TV, newspapers, etc.) used to promote the institution.

| Very | Often | Occasionally | Rarely | Never |
|------|-------|--------------|--------|-------|
| ❑ | ❑ | ❑ | ❑ | ❑ |

6. Parents are engaged in the recruitment process—either on or off campus—in a meaningful way.

| Very | Often | Occasionally | Rarely | Never |
|------|-------|--------------|--------|-------|
| ❑ | ❑ | ❑ | ❑ | ❑ |

7. Students already enrolled are used to recruit other students, targeting the high schools from which they were graduated.

| Very | Often | Occasionally | Rarely | Never |
|------|-------|--------------|--------|-------|
| ❑ | ❑ | ❑ | ❑ | ❑ |

8. The institution uses tests as diagnostic indicators rather than as selective indicators.

| Very | Often | Occasionally | Rarely | Never |
|------|-------|--------------|--------|-------|
| ❑ | ❑ | ❑ | ❑ | ❑ |

9. Admissions criteria are flexible.

| Very | Often | Occasionally | Rarely | Never |
|------|-------|--------------|--------|-------|
| ❑ | ❑ | ❑ | ❑ | ❑ |

10. Ethnic-focused brochures are used in recruiting.

| Very | Often | Occasionally | Rarely | Never |
|------|-------|--------------|--------|-------|
| ❑ | ❑ | ❑ | ❑ | ❑ |

11. Ethnic student representation adequately reflects their proportion in the general population.

| Very | Often | Occasionally | Rarely | Never |
|------|-------|--------------|--------|-------|
| ❑ | ❑ | ❑ | ❑ | ❑ |

Comments_____

## III. FINANCIAL ASSISTANCE

1. The institution uses internal funds to supplement federal dollars.

| Very | Often | Occasionally | Rarely | Never |
|------|-------|--------------|--------|-------|
| ❑ | ❑ | ❑ | ❑ | ❑ |

2. Money is set aside from a restricted general fund to provide grants.

| Very | Often | Occasionally | Rarely | Never |
|------|-------|--------------|--------|-------|
| ❑ | ❑ | ❑ | ❑ | ❑ |

3. Workshops are conducted on budgeting, money management, and alternative financial aid sources for students and parents.

| Very | Often | Occasionally | Rarely | Never |
|------|-------|--------------|--------|-------|
| ❑ | ❑ | ❑ | ❑ | ❑ |

4. The institution makes a conscious effort to minimize the loan debt of low income students through creative strategies such as in-house loans and parent loan programs at low interest rates.

| Very | Often | Occasionally | Rarely | Never |
|------|-------|--------------|--------|-------|
| ❑ | ❑ | ❑ | ❑ | ❑ |

5. Special scholarships are available to high-ranking students of color.

| Very | Often | Occasionally | Rarely | Never |
|------|-------|--------------|--------|-------|
| ❑ | ❑ | ❑ | ❑ | ❑ |

6. The institution offers an extended payment plan for low-income students.

| Very | Often | Occasionally | Rarely | Never |
|------|-------|--------------|--------|-------|
| ❑ | ❑ | ❑ | ❑ | ❑ |

7. Special fundraising programs and campaigns are conducted to secure funds for students of color.

| Very | Often | Occasionally | Rarely | Never |
|------|-------|--------------|--------|-------|
| ❑ | ❑ | ❑ | ❑ | ❑ |

8. Students are assisted in securing employment both on and off campus.

| Very | Often | Occasionally | Rarely | Never |
|------|-------|--------------|--------|-------|
| ❑ | ❑ | ❑ | ❑ | ❑ |

9. Discretionary funds are available to students in emergency situations.

| Very | Often | Occasionally | Rarely | Never |
|------|-------|--------------|--------|-------|
| ❑ | ❑ | ❑ | ❑ | ❑ |

10. The institution conducts exit interviews to determine the impact of the financial aid factor of the student's departure.

| Very | Often | Occasionally | Rarely | Never |
|------|-------|--------------|--------|-------|
| ❑ | ❑ | ❑ | ❑ | ❑ |

Comments_____

## IV. STUDENT SUPPORT SERVICES

1. The institution sponsors workshops to help students of color assess their personal goals.

| Very | Often | Occasionally | Rarely | Never |
|------|-------|--------------|--------|-------|
| ❑ | ❑ | ❑ | ❑ | ❑ |

2. Programs are offered to help new culturally different students become active in the campus community.

| Very | Often | Occasionally | Rarely | Never |
|------|-------|--------------|--------|-------|
| ❑ | ❑ | ❑ | ❑ | ❑ |

3. Students of color make use of the counseling center.

| Very | Often | Occasionally | Rarely | Never |
|------|-------|--------------|--------|-------|
| ❑ | ❑ | ❑ | ❑ | ❑ |

4. Students are enlisted as peer advisors to assist the faculty with the advising program.

| Very | Often | Occasionally | Rarely | Never |
|------|-------|--------------|--------|-------|
| ❑ | ❑ | ❑ | ❑ | ❑ |

5. The placement and career center attracts students of color.

| Very | Often | Occasionally | Rarely | Never |
|------|-------|--------------|--------|-------|
| ❑ | ❑ | ❑ | ❑ | ❑ |

6. Students of color are active in student organizations.

| Very | Often | Occasionally | Rarely | Never |
|------|-------|--------------|--------|-------|
| ❑ | ❑ | ❑ | ❑ | ❑ |

7. A structured procedure has been developed to assess the strengths and skills of disadvantaged students.

| Very | Often | Occasionally | Rarely | Never |
|------|-------|--------------|--------|-------|
| ❑ | ❑ | ❑ | ❑ | ❑ |

8. Special mechanisms are used to assess and screen potential counselors for their ability to work with diverse populations.

| Very | Often | Occasionally | Rarely | Never |
|------|-------|--------------|--------|-------|
| ❑ | ❑ | ❑ | ❑ | ❑ |

9. The institution provides mentors for all students who need special help.

| Very | Often | Occasionally | Rarely | Never |
|------|-------|--------------|--------|-------|
| ❑ | ❑ | ❑ | ❑ | ❑ |

10. Input is sought from constituents of color before programs are put in place that affect them.

| Very | Often | Occasionally | Rarely | Never |
|------|-------|--------------|--------|-------|
| ❑ | ❑ | ❑ | ❑ | ❑ |

11. Support services for students of color have a funding base that promotes stability.

| Very | Often | Occasionally | Rarely | Never |
|------|-------|--------------|--------|-------|
| ❑ | ❑ | ❑ | ❑ | ❑ |

12. Tutoring is available on a walk-in basis.

| Very | Often | Occasionally | Rarely | Never |
|------|-------|--------------|--------|-------|
| ❑ | ❑ | ❑ | ❑ | ❑ |

Comments_____

## V. Curriculum

1. Textbooks are selected that reflect the contributions of persons of various ethnic cultures.

| Very | Often | Occasionally | Rarely | Never |
|------|-------|--------------|--------|-------|
| ❑ | ❑ | ❑ | ❑ | ❑ |

2. Curriculum reform measures have been established to create courses that will expose students to new knowledge about ethnic minorities.

| Very | Often | Occasionally | Rarely | Never |
|------|-------|--------------|--------|-------|
| ❑ | ❑ | ❑ | ❑ | ❑ |

3. Majority students are encouraged to enroll in ethnic-focused courses.

| Very | Often | Occasionally | Rarely | Never |
|------|-------|--------------|--------|-------|
| ❑ | ❑ | ❑ | ❑ | ❑ |

4. Teaching throughout the institution is sensitive to multicultural issues and concerns.

| Very | Often | Occasionally | Rarely | Never |
|------|-------|--------------|--------|-------|
| ❑ | ❑ | ❑ | ❑ | ❑ |

5. The institution promotes the use of educational television as a mechanism for helping students to learn more about pluralism.

| Very | Often | Occasionally | Rarely | Never |
|------|-------|--------------|--------|-------|
| ❑ | ❑ | ❑ | ❑ | ❑ |

6. Holdings in the library and bookstore reflect expanding support for multicultural curricula.

| Very | Often | Occasionally | Rarely | Never |
|------|-------|--------------|--------|-------|
| ❑ | ❑ | ❑ | ❑ | ❑ |

7. Ethnic study courses are a part of the required core curriculum.

| Very | Often | Occasionally | Rarely | Never |
|------|-------|--------------|--------|-------|
| ❑ | ❑ | ❑ | ❑ | ❑ |

8. Workshops are conducted to train faculty how to expand and strengthen their courses to reflect a multicultural perspective.

| Very | Often | Occasionally | Rarely | Never |
|------|-------|--------------|--------|-------|
| ❑ | ❑ | ❑ | ❑ | ❑ |

9. Mechanisms have been put in place to assess the diversity of institutional curricula on a regular basis.

| Very | Often | Occasionally | Rarely | Never |
|------|-------|--------------|--------|-------|
| ❑ | ❑ | ❑ | ❑ | ❑ |

10. The institution encourages research (term papers, essays, etc.) on multicultural issues.

| Very | Often | Occasionally | Rarely | Never |
|------|-------|--------------|--------|-------|
| ❑ | ❑ | ❑ | ❑ | ❑ |

Comments_____

## VI. CAMPUS ENVIRONMENT

1. Administrators meet with faculty and students of color to learn of their interests and concerns.

| Very | Often | Occasionally | Rarely | Never |
|------|-------|--------------|--------|-------|
| ❑ | ❑ | ❑ | ❑ | ❑ |

2. Administrators and faculty set aside time to attend multicultural events.

| Very | Often | Occasionally | Rarely | Never |
|------|-------|--------------|--------|-------|
| ❑ | ❑ | ❑ | ❑ | ❑ |

3. The institution expects students of color to succeed, and develops strategies to help them do so.

| Very | Often | Occasionally | Rarely | Never |
|------|-------|--------------|--------|-------|
| ❑ | ❑ | ❑ | ❑ | ❑ |

4. Institutional initiatives are developed and implemented to promote racial awareness and sensitivity to multicultural issues.

| Very | Often | Occasionally | Rarely | Never |
|------|-------|--------------|--------|-------|
| ❑ | ❑ | ❑ | ❑ | ❑ |

5. A conscious effort is made to involve college personnel in ethnic minority community organizations.

| Very | Often | Occasionally | Rarely | Never |
|------|-------|--------------|--------|-------|
| ❑ | ❑ | ❑ | ❑ | ❑ |

6. Weekend programs and projects are established to involve local (off campus) youth of color and to acquaint them with college resources.

| Very | Often | Occasionally | Rarely | Never |
|------|-------|--------------|--------|-------|
| ❑ | ❑ | ❑ | ❑ | ❑ |

7. Students of color have a center or "family room" area where they can feel comfortable and share common interests and concerns.

| Very | Often | Occasionally | Rarely | Never |
|------|-------|--------------|--------|-------|
| ❏ | ❏ | ❏ | ❏ | ❏ |

8. The institution recognizes eminent leaders and alumni of color by naming buildings, scholarships, lectureships in their honor and by awarding them honorary degrees.

| Very | Often | Occasionally | Rarely | Never |
|------|-------|--------------|--------|-------|
| ❏ | ❏ | ❏ | ❏ | ❏ |

9. Scholars and artists of color are invited to the campus to participate in campus events.

| Very | Often | Occasionally | Rarely | Never |
|------|-------|--------------|--------|-------|
| ❏ | ❏ | ❏ | ❏ | ❏ |

10. Students of color are encouraged to participate in campus organizations.

| Very | Often | Occasionally | Rarely | Never |
|------|-------|--------------|--------|-------|
| ❏ | ❏ | ❏ | ❏ | ❏ |

11. Students are encouraged to form their own support groups to provide opportunities for education and social interaction.

| Very | Often | Occasionally | Rarely | Never |
|------|-------|--------------|--------|-------|
| ❏ | ❏ | ❏ | ❏ | ❏ |

Comments_____

## VII. GRADUATE AND PROFESSIONAL PROGRAMS

1. The institution uses qualifying test scores (GRE, GMAT, LSAT, MCAT, etc.) as a major instrument of selection.

| Very | Often | Occasionally | Rarely | Never |
|------|-------|--------------|--------|-------|
| ❏ | ❏ | ❏ | ❏ | ❏ |

2. The institution includes non-cognitive factors in considering the admissibility of students of color.

| Very | Often | Occasionally | Rarely | Never |
|------|-------|--------------|--------|-------|
| ❏ | ❏ | ❏ | ❏ | ❏ |

3. Linkages between the institution and historical institutions of color are established to assist in recruiting students of color.

| Very | Often | Occasionally | Rarely | Never |
|------|-------|--------------|--------|-------|
| ❑ | ❑ | ❑ | ❑ | ❑ |

4. Faculty and graduates of color are used to recruit prospective graduate and professional students of color.

| Very | Often | Occasionally | Rarely | Never |
|------|-------|--------------|--------|-------|
| ❑ | ❑ | ❑ | ❑ | ❑ |

5. A mechanism is in place to target undergraduate students of color within the institution and make them aware of graduate opportunities available on campus.

| Very | Often | Occasionally | Rarely | Never |
|------|-------|--------------|--------|-------|
| ❑ | ❑ | ❑ | ❑ | ❑ |

6. Fellowships and assistantships have been designated for students of color.

| Very | Often | Occasionally | Rarely | Never |
|------|-------|--------------|--------|-------|
| ❑ | ❑ | ❑ | ❑ | ❑ |

7. Visitation programs are a part of the institution's graduate and professional recruitment efforts.

| Very | Often | Occasionally | Rarely | Never |
|------|-------|--------------|--------|-------|
| ❑ | ❑ | ❑ | ❑ | ❑ |

8. Faculty are trained to be aware of multicultural issues and to serve as mentors for students of color.

| Very | Often | Occasionally | Rarely | Never |
|------|-------|--------------|--------|-------|
| ❑ | ❑ | ❑ | ❑ | ❑ |

9. Students of color are advised to form interest groups in the area of their academic concentration for peer support.

| Very | Often | Occasionally | Rarely | Never |
|------|-------|--------------|--------|-------|
| ❑ | ❑ | ❑ | ❑ | ❑ |

10. Special incentives are available to departments that have innovative projects to recruit and retain people of color.

| Very | Often | Occasionally | Rarely | Never |
|------|-------|--------------|--------|-------|
| ❑ | ❑ | ❑ | ❑ | ❑ |

Comments_____

## VIII. MULTICULTURAL HIRING

1. A system of incentives has been provided to attract and retain teachers of color.

| Very | Often | Occasionally | Rarely | Never |
|------|-------|--------------|--------|-------|
| ❑ | ❑ | ❑ | ❑ | ❑ |

2. The institution makes time for teachers of color to pursue research beyond the requirements of the classroom.

| Very | Often | Occasionally | Rarely | Never |
|------|-------|--------------|--------|-------|
| ❑ | ❑ | ❑ | ❑ | ❑ |

3. A "grow your own" strategy is underway to identify bright graduate students of color and fund them for doctoral work before assigning them teaching responsibilities.

| Very | Often | Occasionally | Rarely | Never |
|------|-------|--------------|--------|-------|
| ❑ | ❑ | ❑ | ❑ | ❑ |

4. There is a strong effort to seek employment for the spouse of a faculty member who has been hired by the institution.

| Very | Often | Occasionally | Rarely | Never |
|------|-------|--------------|--------|-------|
| ❑ | ❑ | ❑ | ❑ | ❑ |

5. Faculty and/or staff of color are involved in searches.

| Very | Often | Occasionally | Rarely | Never |
|------|-------|--------------|--------|-------|
| ❑ | ❑ | ❑ | ❑ | ❑ |

6. Senior faculty are assigned as mentors to junior faculty of color.

| Very | Often | Occasionally | Rarely | Never |
|------|-------|--------------|--------|-------|
| ❑ | ❑ | ❑ | ❑ | ❑ |

7. Special funds are available to faculty of color for professional development.

| Very | Often | Occasionally | Rarely | Never |
|------|-------|--------------|--------|-------|
| ❑ | ❑ | ❑ | ❑ | ❑ |

8. The institution recognizes and gives credit to faculty of color who wish to gain skills that will prepare them for administrative opportunities.

| Very | Often | Occasionally | Rarely | Never |
|------|-------|--------------|--------|-------|
| ❑ | ❑ | ❑ | ❑ | ❑ |

9. Administrative internships are available to personnel of color who wish to gain skills that will prepare them for administrative opportunities.

| Very | Often | Occasionally | Rarely | Never |
|------|-------|--------------|--------|-------|
| ❑ | ❑ | ❑ | ❑ | ❑ |

10. Employee education programs are available to help adult employees of color gain academic skills, pursue college work, and ultimately graduate.

| Very | Often | Occasionally | Rarely | Never |
|------|-------|--------------|--------|-------|
| ❑ | ❑ | ❑ | ❑ | ❑ |

Comments_____

**Appendix D**

# OVERALL STUDENT EXPERIENCE

The instruments contained in this section suggest ways to measure the effectiveness of campus activities, services, and facilities on students' experiences. These tools provide faculty and administrators with insight into the quality of student collegiate experiences inside and outside of the classroom. These instruments encourage students to engage in reflection and self-evaluation. In addition, the instruments highlight areas where modifications and changes on campuses could stimulate greater educational progress.

The assessment tools* in this appendix are:

- College Student Experiences Questionnaire (CSEQ)
- Noncognitive Questionnaire

* All assessment tools are used with permission. Please note that if you decide to use any of the assessment tools, you must obtain a separate copyright permission directly from the author/creator. The copyright holder is listed prior to each tool for your convenience.

# COLLEGE STUDENT EXPERIENCES
# QUESTIONNAIRE

The College Student Experiences Questionnaire (CSEQ) asks students about their progress and the quality of their experiences inside and outside the classroom. In doing so, the CSEQ assesses the quality of effort that college students expend in using the resources and opportunities provided by the institution for their learning and development. Quality of effort is one of the best predictors for understanding college impact because it provides an estimate of the contributions students make to their own learning as well as the resources the institution offers.

The content of the CSEQ is both comprehensive and specific allowing faculty and administrators to see where modifications and changes could stimulate more effort leading to greater educational progress. In addition to providing valuable information for the institution, the CSEQ encourages students to engage in reflection and self-evaluation. Many students have said that filling out the questionnaire prompted them to recall the range of activities in which they participated during the year and the progress they made toward important goals.

For more information on the CSEQ, contact:

George D. Kuh, Director
College Student Experiences Questionnaire Research Program
Center for Postsecondary Research & Planning
Indiana University
1913 East Seventh Street - Ashton Aley 102
Bloomington, IN 47405-7510
Phone: 812-85-5825
Email: cseq@indiana.edu

# COLLEGE STUDENT EXPERIENCES QUESTIONNAIRE

Welcome to the demo version of College Student Experiences Questionnaire. You may fill out the survey normally, but your responses will not be stored in our database.

## *BACKGROUND INFORMATION*

Directions:

Indicate your response by filling in one of the squares under each question.

**Age**
- ❏ 19 or younger
- ❏ 20 - 23
- ❏ 24 - 29
- ❏ 30 - 39
- ❏ 40 - 55
- ❏ Over 55

**Sex**
- ❏ Male
- ❏ Female

**What is your marital status?**
- ❏ Not married
- ❏ Married
- ❏ Divorced/Separated
- ❏ Widowed

**What is your classification in college?**
- ❏ Freshman/first-year
- ❏ Sophomore
- ❏ Junior
- ❏ Senior
- ❏ Graduate student
- ❏ Unclassified

**Did you begin college here or did you transfer here from another institution?**

❑ Started here

❑ Transferred from another institution

**Where do you now live during the school year?**

❑ Dormitory or other campus housing

❑ Residence (house, apartment, etc.) within walking distance of the institution

❑ Residence (house, apartment, etc.) within driving distance

❑ Fraternity or sorority house

**With whom do you live during the school year? (Fill in all boxes that apply)**

❑ No one, I live alone

❑ One or more other students

❑ My spouse or partner

❑ My child or children

❑ My parents

❑ Other relatives

❑ Friends who are not students at the institution I'm attending

❑ Other people: who? _____

**Do you have access to a computer where you live or work, or nearby that you can use for your school work?**

❑ Yes

❑ No

**What have most of your grades been up to now at this institution?**

❑ A

❑ A-,B+

❑ B

❑ B-,C+

❑ C,C-, or lower

**Which of these fields best describes your major, or your anticipated major? (Fill in all boxes that apply)**

❑ Agriculture

❑ Biological/life sciences (biology, biochemistry, botany, zoology, etc.)

❑ Business (accounting, business administration, marketing, management, etc.)

❑ Communication (speech, journalism, television/radio, etc.)

❑ Computer and information sciences

- ❑ Education
- ❑ Engineering
- ❑ Ethnic, cultural studies, and area studies
- ❑ Foreign languages and literature (French, Spanish, etc.)
- ❑ Health-related fields (nursing, physical therapy, health technology, etc.)
- ❑ History
- ❑ Humanities (English, literature, philosophy, religion, etc.)
- ❑ Liberal/general studies
- ❑ Mathematics
- ❑ Multi/interdisciplinary studies (international relations, ecology, environmental studies, etc.)
- ❑ Parks, recreation, leisure studies, sports management
- ❑ Physical sciences (physics, chemistry, astronomy, earth science, etc.)
- ❑ Pre-professional (pre-dental, pre-medical, pre-veterinary)
- ❑ Public administration (city management, law enforcement, etc.)
- ❑ Social sciences (anthropology, economics, political science, psychology, sociology, etc.)
- ❑ Visual and performing arts (art, music, theater, etc.)
- ❑ Undecided
- ❑ Other:

**Did either of your parents graduate from college?**
- ❑ No
- ❑ Yes, both parents
- ❑ Yes, father only
- ❑ Yes, mother only
- ❑ Don't know

**Do you expect to enroll for an advanced degree when, or if, you complete your undergraduate degree?**
- ❑ Yes
- ❑ No

**How many credit hours are you taking this term?**
- ❑ 6 or fewer
- ❑ 7-11
- ❑ 12-14
- ❑ 15-16
- ❑ 17 or more

During the time school is in session, about how many hours a week do you usually spend outside of class on activities related to your academic program, such as studying, writing, reading, lab work, rehearsing, etc.?

❑  5 or fewer hours a week

❑  6 - 10 hours a week

❑  11 - 15 hours a week

❑  16 - 20 hours a week

❑  21 - 25 hours a week

❑  26 - 30 hours a week

❑  More than 30 hours a week

About how many hours do you spend in a typical week doing each of the following?

|  | I don't work | 1-10 hours | 11-20 hours | 21-30 hours | 31-40 hours | More than 40 hours |
|---|---|---|---|---|---|---|
| Working for pay on campus | ❑ | ❑ | ❑ | ❑ | ❑ | ❑ |
| Working for pay off campus | ❑ | ❑ | ❑ | ❑ | ❑ | ❑ |

If you have a job, how does it affect your school work?

❑  I don't have a job

❑  My job does not interfere with my school work

❑  My job takes some time from my school work

❑  My job takes a lot of time from my school work

How do you meet your college expenses? Fill in the response that best approximates the amount of support from each of the various sources.

|  | None | Very Little | Less than half | About half | More than half | All or nearly all |
|---|---|---|---|---|---|---|
| Self (job, savings, etc) | ❑ | ❑ | ❑ | ❑ | ❑ | ❑ |
| Parents | ❑ | ❑ | ❑ | ❑ | ❑ | ❑ |
| Spouse or partner | ❑ | ❑ | ❑ | ❑ | ❑ | ❑ |
| Employer support | ❑ | ❑ | ❑ | ❑ | ❑ | ❑ |
| Scholarships and grants | ❑ | ❑ | ❑ | ❑ | ❑ | ❑ |
| Other sources | ❑ | ❑ | ❑ | ❑ | ❑ | ❑ |

What is your racial or ethnic identification? (Fill in all boxes that apply)

❑  American Indian or other Native American

❑  Asian or Pacific Islander

❑  Black or African American

❑  White (other than Hispanic)

❑ Mexican-American
❑ Puerto Rican
❑ Other Hispanic
❑ Other: _____

## COLLEGE ACTIVITIES

Directions:

During the current school year at this institution, about how often have you done each of the following?

### Library

| | Very | Often | Occasionally | Rarely | Never |
|---|---|---|---|---|---|
| Used library as a quiet place to read or study materials you brought with you. | ❑ | ❑ | ❑ | ❑ | ❑ |
| Found something interesting while browsing in the library. | ❑ | ❑ | ❑ | ❑ | ❑ |
| Asked a librarian or staff member for help in finding information on some topic. | ❑ | ❑ | ❑ | ❑ | ❑ |
| Read assigned materials other than textbooks in the library (reserve readings, etc.). | ❑ | ❑ | ❑ | ❑ | ❑ |
| Used an index or database (computer, card catalog, etc.) to find material on some topic. | ❑ | ❑ | ❑ | ❑ | ❑ |
| Developed a bibliography or reference list for a term paper or other report. | ❑ | ❑ | ❑ | ❑ | ❑ |
| Gone back to read a basic reference or document that other authors referred to. | ❑ | ❑ | ❑ | ❑ | ❑ |
| Made a judgment about the quality of information obtained from the library, World Wide Web, or other sources. | ❑ | ❑ | ❑ | ❑ | ❑ |

Directions:

Again, during the current school year at this institution, about how often have you done each of the following?

**Computer and Information Technology**

| | Very | Often | Occasionally | Rarely | Never |
|---|---|---|---|---|---|
| Used a computer or word processor to prepare reports or papers. | ❑ | ❑ | ❑ | ❑ | ❑ |
| Used e-mail to communicate with an instructor or other students. | ❑ | ❑ | ❑ | ❑ | ❑ |
| Used a computer tutorial to learn material for a course or developmental/remedial program. | ❑ | ❑ | ❑ | ❑ | ❑ |
| Participated in class discussions using an electronic medium (e-mail, list-serve, chat group, etc.). | ❑ | ❑ | ❑ | ❑ | ❑ |
| Searched the Internet for material related to a course. | ❑ | ❑ | ❑ | ❑ | ❑ |
| Used a computer to retrieve materials from a library not at this institution. | ❑ | ❑ | ❑ | ❑ | ❑ |
| Used a computer to produce visual displays of information (charts, graphs, spreadsheets, etc.). | ❑ | ❑ | ❑ | ❑ | ❑ |
| Used a computer to analyze data (statistics, forecasting, etc.). | ❑ | ❑ | ❑ | ❑ | ❑ |
| Developed a Web page or multi-media presentation. | ❑ | ❑ | ❑ | ❑ | ❑ |

Directions:

About how often have you done each of the following?

**Course Learning**

| | Very | Often | Occasionally | Rarely | Never |
|---|---|---|---|---|---|
| Completed the assigned readings for the class. | ❑ | ❑ | ❑ | ❑ | ❑ |
| Took detailed notes during class. | ❑ | ❑ | ❑ | ❑ | ❑ |
| Contributed to class discussions. | ❑ | ❑ | ❑ | ❑ | ❑ |
| Developed a role play, case study, or simulation for a class. | ❑ | ❑ | ❑ | ❑ | ❑ |
| Tried to see how different facts and ideas fit together. | ❑ | ❑ | ❑ | ❑ | ❑ |
| Summarized major points and information from your class notes or readings. | ❑ | ❑ | ❑ | ❑ | ❑ |
| Worked on a class assignment, project, or presentation with other students. | ❑ | ❑ | ❑ | ❑ | ❑ |
| Applied material learned in a class to other areas (your job or internship, other courses, relationships with friends, family, co-workers, etc.). | ❑ | ❑ | ❑ | ❑ | ❑ |
| Used information or experience from other areas of your life (job, internship, interactions with others) in class discussions or assignments. | ❑ | ❑ | ❑ | ❑ | ❑ |
| Tried to explain material from a course to someone else (another student, friend, co-worker, family member). | ❑ | ❑ | ❑ | ❑ | ❑ |
| Worked on a paper or project where you had to integrate ideas from various sources. | ❑ | ❑ | ❑ | ❑ | ❑ |

Directions:

About how often have you done each of the following?

**Writing Experiences**

| | Very | Often | Occasionally | Rarely | Never |
|---|---|---|---|---|---|
| Used a dictionary or thesaurus to look up the proper meaning of words. | ❏ | ❏ | ❏ | ❏ | ❏ |
| Thought about grammar, sentence structure, word choice, and sequence of ideas or points as you were writing. | ❏ | ❏ | ❏ | ❏ | ❏ |
| Asked other people to read something you wrote to see if it was clear to them. | ❏ | ❏ | ❏ | ❏ | ❏ |
| Referred to a book or manual about writing style, grammar, etc. | ❏ | ❏ | ❏ | ❏ | ❏ |
| Revised a paper or composition two or more times before you were satisfied with it. | ❏ | ❏ | ❏ | ❏ | ❏ |
| Asked an instructor or staff member for advice and help to improve your writing. | ❏ | ❏ | ❏ | ❏ | ❏ |
| Prepared a major written report for a class (20 pages or more). | ❏ | ❏ | ❏ | ❏ | ❏ |

Directions:

About how often have you done each of the following?

**Experiences with Faculty**

| | Very | Often | Occasionally | Rarely | Never |
|---|---|---|---|---|---|
| Talked with your instructor about information related to a course you were taking (grades, make-up work, assignments, etc.). | ❑ | ❑ | ❑ | ❑ | ❑ |
| Discussed your academic program or course selection with a faculty member. | ❑ | ❑ | ❑ | ❑ | ❑ |
| Discussed ideas for a term paper or other class project with a faculty member. | ❑ | ❑ | ❑ | ❑ | ❑ |
| Discussed your career plans and ambitions with a faculty member. | ❑ | ❑ | ❑ | ❑ | ❑ |
| Worked harder as a result of feedback from an instructor. | ❑ | ❑ | ❑ | ❑ | ❑ |
| Socialized with a faculty member outside of class (had a snack or soft drink, etc.). | ❑ | ❑ | ❑ | ❑ | ❑ |
| Participated with other students in a discussion with one or more faculty members outside of class. | ❑ | ❑ | ❑ | ❑ | ❑ |
| Asked your instructor for comments and criticisms about your academic performance. | ❑ | ❑ | ❑ | ❑ | ❑ |
| Worked harder than you thought you could to meet an instructor's expectations and standards. | ❑ | ❑ | ❑ | ❑ | ❑ |
| Worked with a faculty member on a research project. | ❑ | ❑ | ❑ | ❑ | ❑ |

Directions:

Again, during the current school year at this institution, about how often have you done each of the following?

**Art, Music, Theater**

| | Very | Often | Occasionally | Rarely | Never |
|---|---|---|---|---|---|
| Talked about art (painting, sculpture, artists, etc.) or the theater (plays, musicals, dance, etc.) with other students, friends, or family members. | ❑ | ❑ | ❑ | ❑ | ❑ |
| Went to art exhibit/gallery or a play, dance, or other theater performance, on or off the campus. | ❑ | ❑ | ❑ | ❑ | ❑ |
| Participated in some art activity (painting, pottery, weaving, drawing, etc.) or theater event, or worked on some theatrical production (acted, danced, worked on scenery, etc.), on or off the campus. | ❑ | ❑ | ❑ | ❑ | ❑ |
| Talked about music or musicians (classical, popular, etc.) with other students, friends, or family members. | ❑ | ❑ | ❑ | ❑ | ❑ |
| Attended a concert or other music event, on or off the campus. | ❑ | ❑ | ❑ | ❑ | ❑ |
| Participated in some music activity (orchestra, chorus, dance, etc.) on or off the campus. | ❑ | ❑ | ❑ | ❑ | ❑ |
| Read or discussed the opinions of art, music, or drama critics. | ❑ | ❑ | ❑ | ❑ | ❑ |

Directions:

About how often have you done each of the following?

**Campus Facilities**

| | Very | Often | Occasionally | Rarely | Never |
|---|---|---|---|---|---|
| Used a campus lounge to relax or study by yourself. | ❑ | ❑ | ❑ | ❑ | ❑ |
| Met other students at some campus location (campus center, etc.) for a discussion. | ❑ | ❑ | ❑ | ❑ | ❑ |
| Attended a cultural or social event in the campus center or other campus location. | ❑ | ❑ | ❑ | ❑ | ❑ |
| Went to lecture or panel discussion. | ❑ | ❑ | ❑ | ❑ | ❑ |
| Used a campus learning lab or center to improve study or academic skills (reading, writing, etc.). | ❑ | ❑ | ❑ | ❑ | ❑ |
| Used campus recreational facilities (pool, fitness equipment, courts, etc.). | ❑ | ❑ | ❑ | ❑ | ❑ |
| Played a team sport (intramural, club, intercollegiate). | ❑ | ❑ | ❑ | ❑ | ❑ |
| Followed a regular schedule of exercise or practice for some recreational sporting activity. | ❑ | ❑ | ❑ | ❑ | ❑ |

Directions:

About how often have you done each of the following?

**Clubs and Organizations**

| | Very | Often | Occasionally | Rarely | Never |
|---|---|---|---|---|---|
| Attended a meeting of a campus club, organization, or student government group. | ❏ | ❏ | ❏ | ❏ | ❏ |
| Worked on a campus committee, student organization, or project (publications, student government, special event, etc.). | ❏ | ❏ | ❏ | ❏ | ❏ |
| Worked on an off-campus committee, organization, or project (civic group, church group, community event, etc.). | ❏ | ❏ | ❏ | ❏ | ❏ |
| Met with a faculty member or staff advisor to discuss the activities of a group or organization. | ❏ | ❏ | ❏ | ❏ | ❏ |
| Managed or provided leadership for a club or organization, on or off the campus. | ❏ | ❏ | ❏ | ❏ | ❏ |

Directions:

About how often have you done each of the following?

**Personal Experiences**

| | Very | Often | Occasionally | Rarely | Never |
|---|---|---|---|---|---|
| Told a friend or family member why you reacted to another person the way you did. | ❏ | ❏ | ❏ | ❏ | ❏ |
| Discussed with another student, friend, or family member why some people get along smoothly, and others do not. | ❏ | ❏ | ❏ | ❏ | ❏ |
| Asked a friend for help with a personal problem. | ❏ | ❏ | ❏ | ❏ | ❏ |
| Read articles or books about personal growth, self-improvement, or social development. | ❏ | ❏ | ❏ | ❏ | ❏ |
| Identified with a character in a book, movie, or television show and wondered what you might have done under similar circumstances. | ❏ | ❏ | ❏ | ❏ | ❏ |
| Taken a test to measure your abilities, interests, or attitudes. | ❏ | ❏ | ❏ | ❏ | ❏ |
| Asked a friend to tell you what he or she really thought about you. | ❏ | ❏ | ❏ | ❏ | ❏ |
| Talked with a faculty member, counselor or other staff member about personal concerns. | ❏ | ❏ | ❏ | ❏ | ❏ |

Directions:

During the current school year at this institution, about how often have you done each of the following?

**Student Acquaintances**

| | Very | Often | Occasionally | Rarely | Never |
|---|:---:|:---:|:---:|:---:|:---:|
| Became acquainted with students whose interests were different from yours. | ❑ | ❑ | ❑ | ❑ | ❑ |
| Became acquainted with students whose family background (economic, social) was different from yours. | ❑ | ❑ | ❑ | ❑ | ❑ |
| Became acquainted with students whose age was different from yours. | ❑ | ❑ | ❑ | ❑ | ❑ |
| Became acquainted with students whose race or ethic background was different from yours. | ❑ | ❑ | ❑ | ❑ | ❑ |
| Became acquainted with students from another country. | ❑ | ❑ | ❑ | ❑ | ❑ |
| Had serious discussions with students whose philosophy of life or personal values were very different from yours. | ❑ | ❑ | ❑ | ❑ | ❑ |
| Had serious discussions with students whose political opinions were very different from yours. | ❑ | ❑ | ❑ | ❑ | ❑ |
| Had serious discussions with students whose religious beliefs were very different from yours. | ❑ | ❑ | ❑ | ❑ | ❑ |
| Had serious discussions with students whose race or ethnic background was different from yours. | ❑ | ❑ | ❑ | ❑ | ❑ |
| Had serious discussions with students from a country different from yours. | ❑ | ❑ | ❑ | ❑ | ❑ |

Directions:

About how often have you done each of the following?

## Scientific and Quantitative Experiences

| | Very | Often | Occasionally | Rarely | Never |
|---|---|---|---|---|---|
| Memorized formulas, definitions, technical terms and concepts. | ❏ | ❏ | ❏ | ❏ | ❏ |
| Used mathematical terms to express a set of relationships. | ❏ | ❏ | ❏ | ❏ | ❏ |
| Explained your understanding of some scientific or mathematical theory, principle or concept to someone else (classmate, co-worker, etc.). | ❏ | ❏ | ❏ | ❏ | ❏ |
| Read articles about scientific or mathematical theories or concepts in addition to those assigned for a class. | ❏ | ❏ | ❏ | ❏ | ❏ |
| Completed an experiment or project using scientific methods. | ❏ | ❏ | ❏ | ❏ | ❏ |
| Practiced to improve your skill in using a piece of laboratory equipment. | ❏ | ❏ | ❏ | ❏ | ❏ |
| Showed someone else how to use a piece of scientific equipment. | ❏ | ❏ | ❏ | ❏ | ❏ |
| Explained an experimental procedure to someone else. | ❏ | ❏ | ❏ | ❏ | ❏ |
| Compared the scientific method with other methods for gaining knowledge and understanding. | ❏ | ❏ | ❏ | ❏ | ❏ |
| Explained to another person the scientific basis for concerns about scientific or environmental issues (pollution, recycling, alternative sources of energy, acid rain) or similar aspects of the world around you. | ❏ | ❏ | ❏ | ❏ | ❏ |

## CONVERSATIONS

Directions:

In conversations with others (students, family members, co-workers, etc.) outside the classroom during this school year, about how often have you talked about each of the following?

### Topics of Conversation

| | Very | Often | Occasionally | Rarely | Never |
|---|---|---|---|---|---|
| Current events in the news. | ❏ | ❏ | ❏ | ❏ | ❏ |
| Social issues such as peace, justice, human rights, equality, race relations. | ❏ | ❏ | ❏ | ❏ | ❏ |
| Different lifestyles, customs, and religions. | ❏ | ❏ | ❏ | ❏ | ❏ |
| The ideas and views of other people such as writers, philosophers, historians. | ❏ | ❏ | ❏ | ❏ | ❏ |
| The arts (painting, poetry, dance, theatrical productions, symphony, movies, etc.). | ❏ | ❏ | ❏ | ❏ | ❏ |
| Science (theories, experiments, methods, etc.). | ❏ | ❏ | ❏ | ❏ | ❏ |
| Computers and other technologies. | ❏ | ❏ | ❏ | ❏ | ❏ |
| Social and ethical issues related to science and technology such as energy, pollution, chemicals, genetics, military use. | ❏ | ❏ | ❏ | ❏ | ❏ |
| The economy (employment, wealth, poverty, debt, trade, etc.). | ❏ | ❏ | ❏ | ❏ | ❏ |
| International relations (human rights, free trade, military activities, political differences, etc.). | ❏ | ❏ | ❏ | ❏ | ❏ |

Directions:

In conversations with others (students, family members, co-workers, etc.) outside the classroom during this school year, about how often have you talked about each of the following?

**Information in Conversations**

|  | Very | Often | Occasionally | Rarely | Never |
|---|---|---|---|---|---|
| Referred to knowledge you acquired in your reading or classes. | ❑ | ❑ | ❑ | ❑ | ❑ |
| Explored different ways of thinking about the topic. | ❑ | ❑ | ❑ | ❑ | ❑ |
| Referred to something one of your instructors said about the topic. | ❑ | ❑ | ❑ | ❑ | ❑ |
| Subsequently read something that was related to the topic. | ❑ | ❑ | ❑ | ❑ | ❑ |
| Changed your opinion as a result of the knowledge or arguments presented by others. | ❑ | ❑ | ❑ | ❑ | ❑ |
| Persuaded others to change their minds as a result of the knowledge or arguments you cited. | ❑ | ❑ | ❑ | ❑ | ❑ |

## READING/WRITING

During this current year, about how many books have you read? Fill in one response for each item listed below.

|  | None | Fewer than 5 | Between 5 and 10 | Between 11 and 20 | More than 20 |
|---|---|---|---|---|---|
| Textbooks or assigned books | ❑ | ❑ | ❑ | ❑ | ❑ |
| Assigned packs of course readings | ❑ | ❑ | ❑ | ❑ | ❑ |
| Non-assigned books | ❑ | ❑ | ❑ | ❑ | ❑ |

About how many exams, papers, or reports have you written? Fill in one response for each item listed below.

|  | None | Fewer than 5 | Between 5 and 10 | Between 11 and 20 | More than 20 |
|---|---|---|---|---|---|
| Essay exams for your courses | ❑ | ❑ | ❑ | ❑ | ❑ |
| Term papers or other written reports | ❑ | ❑ | ❑ | ❑ | ❑ |

## OPINIONS ABOUT YOUR COLLEGE OR UNIVERSITY

How well do you like college?

❑ I am enthusiastic about it.

❑ I like it.

❑ I am more or less neutral about it.

❑ I don't like it.

If you could start over again, would you go to the same institution you are now attending?

❑ Yes, definitely

❑ Probably yes

❑ Probably no

❑ No, definitely

## THE COLLEGE ENVIRONMENT

Colleges and universities differ from one another in the extent to which they emphasize or focus on various aspects of students' development. Thinking of your experience at this institution, to what extent do you feel that each of the following is emphasized? The responses are numbered from 7 to 1, with the highest and lowest points illustrated. Fill in the circle with the number that best represents your impression on each of the following seven-point rating scales.

Emphasis on developing academic, scholarly, and intellectual qualities

| Strong Emphasis | | | | | | Weak Emphasis |
|---|---|---|---|---|---|---|
| 7 | 6 | 5 | 4 | 3 | 2 | 1 |
| O | O | O | O | O | O | O |

Emphasis on developing aesthetic, expressive, and creative qualities

| Strong Emphasis | | | | | | Weak Emphasis |
|---|---|---|---|---|---|---|
| 7 | 6 | 5 | 4 | 3 | 2 | 1 |
| O | O | O | O | O | O | O |

Emphasis on developing critical, evaluative, and analytical qualities

| Strong Emphasis | | | | | | Weak Emphasis |
|---|---|---|---|---|---|---|
| 7 | 6 | 5 | 4 | 3 | 2 | 1 |
| O | O | O | O | O | O | O |

Emphasis on developing an understanding and appreciation of human diversity

| Strong Emphasis | | | | | | Weak Emphasis |
|---|---|---|---|---|---|---|
| 7 | 6 | 5 | 4 | 3 | 2 | 1 |
| O | O | O | O | O | O | O |

Emphasis on developing information literacy skills (using computers, other information resources)

Strong Emphasis                                                          Weak Emphasis

| 7 | 6 | 5 | 4 | 3 | 2 | 1 |
|---|---|---|---|---|---|---|
| O | O | O | O | O | O | O |

Emphasis on developing vocational and occupational competence

Strong Emphasis                                                          Weak Emphasis

| 7 | 6 | 5 | 4 | 3 | 2 | 1 |
|---|---|---|---|---|---|---|
| O | O | O | O | O | O | O |

Emphasis on the personal relevance and practical value of your courses

Strong Emphasis                                                          Weak Emphasis

| 7 | 6 | 5 | 4 | 3 | 2 | 1 |
|---|---|---|---|---|---|---|
| O | O | O | O | O | O | O |

The next three ratings refer to relations with people at this college. Again, thinking of your own experience, please rate the quality of these relationships on each of the following seven-point rating scales.

Relationships with other students

Friendly,                                                               Competitive,
Supportive,                                                             Uninvolved,
Sense of belonging                                                      Sense of alienation

| 7 | 6 | 5 | 4 | 3 | 2 | 1 |
|---|---|---|---|---|---|---|
| O | O | O | O | O | O | O |

Relationships with administrative personnel and offices

Helpful,                                                                Rigid,
Considerate,                                                            Impersonal,
Flexible                                                                Bound by regulations

| 7 | 6 | 5 | 4 | 3 | 2 | 1 |
|---|---|---|---|---|---|---|
| O | O | O | O | O | O | O |

Relationships with faculty members

Approachable,                                                           Remote,
Helpful, Understanding,                                                 Discouraging,
Encouraging                                                             Unsympathetic

| 7 | 6 | 5 | 4 | 3 | 2 | 1 |
|---|---|---|---|---|---|---|
| O | O | O | O | O | O | O |

## ESTIMATE OF GAINS

Directions:

In thinking about your college or university experience up to now, to what extent do you feel you have gained or made progress in the following areas?

| | Very Much | Quite a Bit | Some | Very Little |
|---|---|---|---|---|
| Writing clearly and effectively. | ❏ | ❏ | ❏ | ❏ |
| Presenting ideas and information effectively when speaking to others. | ❏ | ❏ | ❏ | ❏ |
| Using computers and other information technologies. | ❏ | ❏ | ❏ | ❏ |
| Becoming aware of different philosophies, cultures, and ways of life. | ❏ | ❏ | ❏ | ❏ |
| Developing your own values and ethical standards. | ❏ | ❏ | ❏ | ❏ |
| Broadening your acquaintance with an enjoyment of literature. | ❏ | ❏ | ❏ | ❏ |
| Seeing the importance of history for understanding the present as well as the past. | ❏ | ❏ | ❏ | ❏ |
| Gaining knowledge about other parts of the world and other people (Asia, Africa, South America, etc.). | ❏ | ❏ | ❏ | ❏ |

Directions:

Again, in thinking about your college or university experience up to now, to what extent do you feel you have gained or made progress in the following areas?

|  | Very Much | Quite a Bit | Some | Very Little |
|---|---|---|---|---|
| Analyzing quantitative problems (understanding probabilities, proportions, etc.). | ❏ | ❏ | ❏ | ❏ |
| Putting ideas together, seeing relationships, similarities, and differences between ideas. | ❏ | ❏ | ❏ | ❏ |
| Learning on your own, pursuing ideas, and finding information you need. | ❏ | ❏ | ❏ | ❏ |
| Learning to adapt to change (new technologies, different jobs or personal circumstances, etc.). | ❏ | ❏ | ❏ | ❏ |
| Understanding the nature of science and experimentation. | ❏ | ❏ | ❏ | ❏ |
| Understanding new developments in science and technology. | ❏ | ❏ | ❏ | ❏ |
| Becoming aware of the consequences (benefits, hazards, dangers) of new applications of science and technology. | ❏ | ❏ | ❏ | ❏ |
| Thinking analytically and logically. | ❏ | ❏ | ❏ | ❏ |

Congratulations! You have completed the survey.

Report Problems:
CSEQ@indiana.edu
Center for Survey Research
1022 E. 3rd St.
Bloomington, IN 47405

# NONCOGNITIVE QUESTIONNAIRE

Colleges and universities typically use cognitive admissions criteria—high school grade point average, standardized test scores, high school curriculum, and class rank—when determining whom to admit. Noncognitive variables, such as letters of recommendation, extracurricular activities, gender, race/ethnicity, socioeconomic status, leadership ability, and disabilities are also considered by admissions officers, but sometimes to a lesser degree. This instrument measures noncognitive variables for the purposes of enhancing admissions procedures. Although used by this institution specifically for admission purposes, this survey can be used to address a variety of campus issues. However, for those campuses interested in using this survey for a similar purpose, a scoring key is attached.

For more information contact:

William Sedlacek
Professor of Education
Assistant Director, Counseling Center
Adjunct Professor of Pharmacy
1101B Shoemaker Bldg.
University of Maryland
College Park, MD 20742-8111
Phone: 301-314-7687
Email: ws12@umail.umd.edu

# COUNSELING CENTER
# UNIVERSITY OF MARYLAND
# COLLEGE PARK, MARYLAND 20742

## SUPPLEMENTARY ADMISSIONS QUESTIONNAIRE II*

The University of Maryland, College Park (UMCP), is trying to improve its admissions procedures by studying additional information about students. Results will be reported for groups only; no individuals will be identified. Please mark your responses on this sheet.

Please fill in the blank or circle the appropriate answers.

1.  Your social security number _____

2.  Your sex is:

    1.  Male
    2. Female

3.  Your age is: _____ years

4.  Your father's occupation:

5.  Your mother's occupation:

6.  Your race is:

    1.  Black (African-American)
    2.  White (not of Hispanic origin)
    3.  Asian (Pacific Islander)
    4.  Hispanic (Latin American)
    5.  American Indian (Alaskan native)
    6.  Other

* See Tracey, T. J., & Sedlacek, W. E. (1984). Noncognitive variables in predicting academic success by race. *Measurement and Evaluation in Guidance, 16,* 171-178, for validity and reliability data.

7.  How much education do you expect to get during your lifetime?

    1.  College, but less than a bachelor's degree
    2.  B.A. or equivalent
    3.  1 or 2 years of graduate or professional study (Master's degree)
    4.  Doctoral degree such as M.D., Ph.D., etc.

8.  Please list three goals that you have for yourself right now:

    1. _____
    2. _____
    3. _____

9. About 50% of university students typically leave before receiving a degree. If this should happen to you, what would be the most likely cause?

    1.  Absolutely certain that I will obtain a degree
    2.  To accept a good job
    3.  To enter military service
    4.  It would cost more than my family could afford
    5.  Marriage
    6.  Disinterest in study
    7.  Lack of academic ability
    8.  Insufficient reading or study skills
    9.  Other

10. Please list three things that you are proud of having done:

    1. _____
    2. _____
    3. _____

Please indicate the extent to which you agree or disagree with each of the following items. Respond to the statements below with your feelings at present or with your expectations of how things will be. Write in your answer to the left of each item.

| 1 | 2 | 3 | 4 | 5 |
|---|---|---|---|---|
| | Strongly | | | Strongly |
| Agree | Agree | Neutral | Disagree | Disagree |

11. The University should use its influence to improve social conditions in the state.

12. It should not be very hard to get a B (3.0) average at UMCP.

13. I get easily discouraged when I try to do something and it doesn't work.

14. I am sometimes looked up to by others.

15. If I run into problems concerning school, I have someone who would listen to me and help me.

16. There is no use in doing things for people, you only find that you get it in the neck in the long run.

17. In groups where I am comfortable, I am often looked to as leader.

18. I expect to have a harder time than most students at UMCP.

19. Once I start something, I finish it.

20. When I believe strongly in something, I act on it.

21. I am as skilled academically as the average applicant to UMCP.

22. I expect I will encounter racism at UMCP.

23. People can pretty easily change me even though I thought my mind was already made up on the subject.

24. My friends and relatives don't feel I should go to college.

25. My family has always wanted me to go to college.

26. If course tutoring is made available on campus at no cost, I would attend regularly.

27. I want a chance to prove myself academically.

28. My high school grades don't really reflect what I can do.

29. Please list offices held and/or groups belonged to in high school or in your community.

**COUNSELING CENTER**
**UNIVERSITY OF MARYLAND**
**COLLEGE PARK, MARYLAND 20742**

## SCORING KEY FOR SUPPLEMENTARY ADMISSIONS
## QUESTIONNAIRE II

William E. Sedlacek

| QUESTIONNAIRE ITEMS | | VARIABLE NAME (NUMBER)<br>Use to score for Self-Concept (I)<br>Option 1 = 1; 2 = 2; 3 = 3; 4 = 4; No response = 2 |
|---|---|---|
| 8 | A. | Options for Long Range Goals (IV)<br>Each goal is coded according to this scheme: |
| | 1 = | a vague and/or immediate, short-term goal (e.g., "to meet people," "to get a good schedule," "to gain self confidence") |
| | 2 = | a specific goal with a stated future orientation which could be accomplished during undergraduate study (e.g., "to join a sorority so I can meet more people," "to get a good schedule so I can get good grades in the fall," "to run for a student government office") |
| | 3 = | a specific goal with a stated future orientation which would occur after undergraduate study (e.g., "to get a good schedule so I can get the classes I need for graduate school;" "to become president of a Fortune 500 company") |
| | B. | Options for Knowledge Acquired in a Field (VIII)<br>Each goal is coded according to this scheme: |
| | 1 = | not at all academically or school related; vague or unclear (e.g., "to get married," "to do better," "to become a better person") |
| | 2 = | school related, but not necessarily or primarily educationally oriented (e.g., "to join a fraternity," "to become student body president") |
| | 3 = | directly related to education (e.g., "to get a 3.5 GPA," "to get to know my teachers") |
| | | Find the mean for each dimension (e.g. Long Range Goals) and round to the nearest whole number. |

| QUESTIONNAIRE ITEMS | VARIABLE NAME (NUMBER) |
|---|---|

9      Use to score for Self-Concept (I) and Self-Appraisal (II)

Option 1 = 4; 2 through 9 = 2; No response = 2

10      Use to score for Self Concept (I)
Each accomplishment is coded according to
this scheme:

1 =      at least 75% of applicants to your school
could have accomplished it (e.g., "graduated from
high school," "held a part-time summer job")

2 =      at least 50% of applicants to your school could have
accomplished it (e.g., played on an intramural sports
team," "was a member of a school club")

3 =      only top 25% of applicants to your school could
have accomplished it (e.g., "won an academic
award," "was captain of football team")

Find the mean code for this dimension and round to the
nearest whole number.

For items 11 through 28, positive (+) items are scored
as is. Negative (-) items are reversed, so that 1 =
5, 2 = 4, 3 = 3, 4 = 2, and 5 = 1. A shortcut is to
subtract all negative item responses from 6.

| QUESTIONNAIRE ITEMS | DIRECTION | VARIABLE NAME (NUMBER) |
|---|---|---|
| 11 | - | Use to score for Racism (III) |
| 12 | - (II) | Use to score for Realistic Self-Appraisal |
| 13 | + | Use to score for Long-Range Goals (IV) |
| 14 | - | Use to score for Leadership (VI) |
| 15 | - | Use to score for Availability of Strong Support (V) |
| 16 | + | Use to score for Community Service (VII) |
| 17 | - | Use to score for Leadership (VI) |
| 18 | + | Use to score for Racism (III) |
| 19 | - | Use to score for Long-Range Goals (IV) |
| 20 | - | Use to score for Positive Self-Concept (I) |
| 21 | - | Use to score for Realistic Self-Appraisal (II) |
| 22 | - | Use to score for Racism (III) |
| 23 | + | Use to score for Positive Self Concept (I) |
| 24 | + | Use to score for Availability of Strong Support (V) |
| 25 | - | Use to score for Availability of Strong Support (V) |
| 26 | - | Use to score for Racism (III) |
| 27 | - | Use to score for Racism (III) |
| 28 | - | Use to score for Positive Self Concept (I) |
| 29 | | Use to score for Leadership (VI), Community |

Service (VII) and Knowledge Acquired in a Field (VIII). Each organization is given a code for A, B, and C below.Find the mean for each dimension (e.g. Leadership) and round to the nearest whole number.

A.      Leadership (VI)

     1 =      ambiguous group or no clear reference to activity performed (e.g., "helped in school")

     2 =      indicates membership but no formal or implied leadership role; it has to be clear that it's a functioning group and, unless the criteria are met for a score of "3" as described below, all groups should be coded as "2" even if you, as the rater, are not familiar with the group (e.g., "Fashionettes," "was part of a group that worked on community service projects through my church")

     3 =      leadership was required to fulfill role in group (e.g., officer or implied initiator, organizer, or founder) or entrance into the group was dependent upon prior leadership (e.g., "organized a tutoring group for underprivileged children in my community," "student council" )

B.      Community Service Relatedness (VII)

     1 =      no community service performed by group, or vague or unclear in relation to community service (e.g., "basketball team").

     2 =      some community service involved but it is not the primary purpose of the group (e.g., "Scouts")

     3 =      group's main purpose is community service (e.g., "Big Brothers/Big Sisters")

C.      Knowledge Acquired in a Field (VIII) (same coding criteria as used for item 8B.)

SUPPLEMENTARY ADMISSIONS QUESTIONNAIRE II
Worksheet for Scoring

1.      POSITIVE SELF-CONCEPT OR CONFIDENCE
item7* + item9* + item10* + (6 - item2O) + item23 + (6 - item28)

2.      REALISTIC SELF-APPRAISAL
item9* + (6 - item12) + (6 - item21)

3.      UNDERSTANDS and DEALS with RACISM
(6 - item11) + item18 + (6 - item22) + (6 - item26) + (6 - item27)

4.          PREFERS LONG-RANGE GOALS to SHORT-
TERM or IMMEDIATE NEEDS
item8A*  +  item13  +  (6 - item19)

5.          AVAILABILITY of a STRONG SUPPORT PERSON
(6 - item15)  +  item24  +  (6 - item25)

6.          SUCCESSFUL LEADERSHIP EXPERIENCE
(6 - item14)  +  (6 - item17)  +  item29A*

7.          DEMONSTRATED COMMUNITY SERVICE
item16  +  item29B*

8.          KNOWLEDGE ACQUIRED in a FIELD
item8B*  +  item29C*

* Recoded item.  See scoring instructions for these items on pages 1-3 herein.

## Appendix E

# INTERVIEW PROTOCOLS

The following questionnaires represent the interview protocols used by external evaluators who were seeking to assess the impact of outside funding agencies that were supporting specific campus diversity initiatives. The first guide is the interview protocol that guided the Lilly Endowment funded initiative, "Improving Racial and Ethnic Diversity and Campus Climate at Four-Year Independent Midwest Colleges." The second is from Philip Morris Companies, Inc. initiative, "Tolerance on Campus: Establishing Common Ground."

The assessment tools* in this appendix are:

- Lilly Endowment Interview Protocol
- Philip Morris Companies Inc. Protocol

* All assessment tools are used with permission. Please note that if you decide to use any of the assessment tools, you must obtain a separate copyright permission directly from the author/creator. The copyright holder is listed prior to each tool for your convenience.

# INTERVIEW PROTOCOL QUESTIONS
# FOR THE LILLY ENDOWMENT EXTERNAL EVALUATIONS

These questions provided the structure for the interviews in the Lilly Endowment evaluation of forty Midwestern colleges from eight states. The interview format addresses principally on perceptions and behaviors since the focus of the grant was to enhance racial and ethnic diversity, build more inclusive communities, and foster understanding of differences.

For more information:

William Sedlacek
Professor of Education
Assistant Director, Counseling Center
Adjunct Professor of Pharmacy
1101B Shoemaker Bldg.
University of Maryland
College Park, MD 20742-8111
Phone:  301-314-7687
Email:  ws12@umail.umd.edu

# LILLY ENDOWMENT
# PROTOCOL QUESTIONS
# EMPLOYED IN CAMPUS SITE VISITS

1. What was the best thing about the program?

2. What was the worst thing about the program?

3. Was the program successful?
   A. Yes                No
   B. How can you tell?  What was your evidence?

4. Long v. short-term effects?

5. What were the goals of the program?
   A. Information
   B. Attitudes
   C. Behavior

6. Noncognitive variables relevant
   A. Self-concept
   B. Realistic self-appraisal
   C. Handling racism
   D. Long-range goals
   E. Leadership
   F. Strong support person
   G. Community involvement
   H. Nontraditional knowledge

7. Audience for Program
   A. Students of color
   B. White students
   C. Faculty of color
   D. White faculty/faculty in general
   E. Program participants only
   F. Those outside program
   G. Staff
      1. Student services
         a. Of color
         b. White
   H. Off Campus

8. Advice for other schools?

9. If you had to do it over?
   A. Would do
   B. Would not do

10. If you had more money?

11. What will happen to program after grant term?

12. Spin-off programs?

13. Who have you left out of the program?

14. How does Lilly Program relate to others you have?

15. How did Lilly Program change after you started?

16. Critical incident
    A. +
    B. −

17. What change at institution would you directly attribute to Lilly grant?
    A. Indirect changes?

18. What changes in the campus climate for diversity now?
    A. +
    B. −

19. Overall impression and anecdotes

20. A way of evaluating I might miss

# PHILIP MORRIS COMPANIES, INC.
# INTERVIEW PROTOCOL QUESTIONS

These questions provided the structure for the interviews in the Philip Morris, Inc. diversity initiative that awarded grants to eleven four-year colleges and universities. The goal of the initiative was to help campuses improve race relations and to create stronger communities of civility and respect. The results of the evaluation are available through the Philip Morris Companies, Inc.

For more information:

Cynthia Hudgins
Senior Research Associate-Social Sciences, School of Social Work
University of Michigan
3743 SSWB 1106
Ann Arbor, MI 48109-1259
Phone: 734-936-8646
Email: hudgins@umich.edu

Or

Michael Nettles
Professor, School of Education
University of Michigan
Center for the Study of Higher and Post-Secondary Education
610 E. University, 2108 SEB
Ann Arbor, MI 48109-1259
Phone: 734-764-9499
Email: nettlesm@umich.edu

# PHILIP MORRIS COMPANIES INC.
## TOLERANCE ON CAMPUS:
## ESTABLISHING COMMON GROUND
## PROTOCOL EMPLOYED IN SITE VISITS

1. What are the primary issues that the project addresses on your campus?

2. What are the central goals of the project?

3. Who is the target audience for the project on your campus?

4. In which campus unit is the project being implemented? Who are the key project personnel and what are their titles? What is their previous experience in such kinds of project oversight?

5. What other efforts are being made on your campus to address diversity issues? How does the project relate to existing campus interventions to address diversity?

6. How would you describe the campus climate in relation to diversity issues prior to receipt of the grant? After receipt of the grant? Do you have archival documents to describe the campus climate (e.g., newspaper clippings, reports)?

7. Why is this project an appropriate fit for your campus at this time?

8. What is the internal evaluation plan for the project? What are the yearly and end of project indicators?

9. How has the project changed from the project design in the original proposal? Why were these changes implemented?

10. What is the actual budget for the project? How has this changed from the proposed budget?

11. What have been barriers to implementation and achieving the objectives of the project? What would you attempt to do differently if you could start again?

12. What are the factors to which you attribute the successful implementation of your project?

13. What would you say are the direct and indirect results (spin-offs) of the project on your campus?

14. What is the relationship of the project to the rest of the campus community? Surrounding community? How has this project assisted with outreach to the neighboring community?

15. What are the plans for sustaining the project upon the completion of the funding cycle? If changes to the original project will be implemented, how were those decided?

16. Given what you have learned through the implementation of your project, what recommendations would you make to foundations funding such kinds of initiatives? To your own campus?

# Appendix F

# EVALUATION RESOURCES

Astin, A.W. 1993. *What matters in college?: Four critical years revisited.* San Francisco: Jossey-Bass.

This massive study uses Astin's input-environment-outcome (I-E-O) model to assess the intellectual and social development and satisfaction with the college experience of over 20,000 students at 200 colleges and universities nationwide. The book examines the effects of 190 environmental variables on student personality, self-concept, attitudes, values, beliefs, patterns of behavior, academic and cognitive development, career development, and satisfaction with college. The chapter on student attitudes, values, and beliefs is of particular interest in the context of diversity research, as is the discussion of policy implications of the research.

Astin, A.W. 1991. *Assessment for excellence. The philosophy and practice of assessment and evaluation in higher education.* New York: American Council on Education/Macmillan.

Astin proposes a new model for measuring excellence based on talent development. Rather than accepting the conventional view that an institution's quality can best be measured by its reputation and its resources, the author suggests a new approach to assessing excellence based on the role that institutions play in the growth and development of students as they move through the institution.

Bowen, W. & Bok, D. 1999. *The shape of the river: Long term consequences of considering race in college and university admissions.* Princeton, NJ: Princeton University Press.

To date, *The Shape of the River* is the most far-reaching and comprehensive study of its kind. It has forever changed the debate on affirmative action in America. This study proves that race-sensitive admissions increase the likelihood that blacks will be admitted to selective universities, and it demonstrates what effect the termination of these policies would have on the enrollment of minority students at many selective institutions.

This book provides a wealth of empirical evidence to demonstrate how race-sensitive admissions policies actually work, and it clearly defines the effects that a diverse student body has had on over 45,000 students of different races.

Fetterman, D.M., Kaftarian, S.J. & Wandersman, A. (Eds.). 1996. *Empowerment evaluation: Knowledge and tools for self-assessment and accountability*. Thousand Oaks, CA: Sage Publishing.

This book provides descriptions of programs that use empowerment evaluation. It offers additional insight into this new evaluation approach, including information about how to conduct workshops that train program staff members and participants to evaluate and improve program practice.

Gurin, P. 1999. New research on the benefits of diversity in colleges and beyond: An empirical analysis. *Diversity digest*. (Spring), 5. http://www.diversityweb.org/Digest/Sp99/benefits.html.

An article based on the author's expert testimony for the defense of the University of Michigan in court proceedings challenging the University's admission policies. From three empirical analyses, Gurin concludes that a diverse campus has far-reaching effects in the intellectual and social development of all students, translating into positive influence for American democracy. Gurin used data from an extensive survey of students at the University of Michigan, multi-institutional national data, and data from a classroom program at the University of Michigan. The three analyses together show the positive relationships between diversity in higher education and learning and democracy outcomes across racial and ethnic groups.

Hurtado, S., Milem, J., Clayton-Pedersen, A., & Allen, W. 1999. Enacting diverse learning environment: Improving the climate for racial/ethnic diversity in higher education. *ASHE-ERIC Higher education report*. (Vol. 26, No. 8). Washington, DC: The George Washington University, Graduate School of Education and Human Development.

In this report, the authors conclude that the key to enacting diverse learning environments lies in understanding and developing programs and policies to improve the campus climate for racial/ethnic diversity. They discuss the importance of assessing the campus climate's impact on students and their learning environment, and offer principles for improving the climate for diversity. Examples of promising practices on campuses are also included.

Loacker, G. (Ed). 2000. *Self-assessment at Alverno College*. Milwaukee, WI: Alverno College.

In this monograph, faculty members of Alverno College describe what they have learned from studying self-assessment as a form of student's learning assessment for more than 25 years. Their focus is on how students experience self-assessment and learn from it in order to improve their academic performance. Faculty from various disciplines explain how self-assessment is applied in their courses.

Moskal, B. M. 2000. Scoring Rubrics: What, When and How? Practical Assessment. *Research & Evaluation*, 7(3). http://ericae.net/pare/getvn.asp?v=7&n=3.

Scoring rubrics have become a common method for evaluating student work in both the K-12 and the college classrooms. The purpose of this paper is to describe the various types of scoring rubrics, explain why scoring rubrics are useful, and provide an outline for developing scoring rubrics. The paper concludes with examples of the different types of scoring rubrics and further guidance on the development process.

Musil, C.M. (Ed.) 1992. *The courage to question: Women's studies and student learning.* Washington, DC: Association of American Colleges and Universities. ERIC, ED 347890.

This book uses seven case studies to assess student learning in women's studies courses. Each of the institutions used a variety of qualitative and quantitative methods to answer some pressing issues about women's studies and student learning on their campus and ultimately to improve the quality of the programs. The assessment documented that women's studies engages students intellectually and personally, re-establishes the centrality of teaching and student-centered learning, and helps students understand different viewpoints and diverse people. Students talk of finding their own voices, engaging in robust debates, and developing critical perspectives.

Musil, C.M. (Ed.) 1992. *Students at the center: Feminist assessment.* Washington, DC: Association of American Colleges and Universities.

The final publication of a three-year research project on women's studies and student learning, *Students at the Center* facilitates program assessment with a focus on feminist principles of assessment. This publication includes innovative assessment designs and practical advice about how to set up a student-centered, faculty-driven assessment project. Useful resources include sample assessment instruments, a directory of consultants, and a selected bibliography.

Musil, C.M., García, M., Moses, Y., & Smith, D.G. 1995. *Diversity in higher education: A work in progress.* Washington, DC: Association of American Colleges and Universities.

In a report commissioned by the Ford Foundation, a team of four evaluators assessed the institutional impact of Ford-funded Campus Diversity Initiatives on nineteen campuses. *Diversity in Higher Education* is not only an assessment of the diversity initiatives, but also assists colleges and universities in making diversity more integral to the mission of higher education. The authors describe the nineteen initiatives, give guidance for institutionalizing project goals, including assessment, and share lessons learned from the diversity initiatives.

Nettles, M.T. & C. Hudgins. 1995. *An evaluation of the Philip Morris Companies, Inc. Tolerance on campus: Establishing common ground initiatives.* New York, NY: Colby College and Northern Illinois University.

These reports were produced for the evaluation component of the Philip Morris Initiative, *Tolerance on Campus: Establishing Common Ground.* The diversity initiative was launched in 1992 with an investment of $1.2 million both to assist Philip Morris in measuring the effectiveness of the initiative to determine the outcomes of the variety of interventions at the eleven participating institutions. Institutions were evaluated using a seven step multidimensional approach, that included two-day site visits, and analysis of qualitative and quantitative data provided by the institutions. Results of both programs proved positive and are described in the context of each report.

Prediger, D.J. 1993. *Multicultural assessment standards: A compilation for counselors.* Alexandria, VA: American Counseling Association.

This compilation of professional standards and guidelines was created by the Association for Assessment in Counseling (AAC), a division of the American Counseling Association (ACA) to further the realization of ACA's special theme for 1993—"Diversity, Development, and Dignity." Although AAC believes that tests, inventories, and other assessment instruments can be beneficial to members of all populations, they recognize that increasing diversity in counselee backgrounds presents special challenges. The standards and guidelines assembled here in this book address many of those challenges.

Sabnani, H.B. & Ponterotto, J.G. 1992. Racial/ethnic minority-specific instrumentation in counseling research: A review, critique, and recommendations. *Measurement and evaluation in counseling and development.* 24(4), 161-187.

This article reviews several instruments specifically developed for use in ethnic, minority-focused psychological research. Instruments and scales include: the African Self-Consciousness Scale; the Cross-Cultural Counseling Inventory-Revised; Modern Racism Scale; Value-Oriented Scale; the Racial Identity Attitude Scale; and the Developmental Inventory of Black Consciousness.

Sedlacek, W.E. 1996. An empirical method of determining nontraditional group status. *Measurement and evaluation in counseling and development.* 28, 200-210.

This article describes the development and application of two assessment techniques, the Noncognitive Questionnaire (NCQ) and the Situational Attitude Scale

(SAS). The noncognitive questionnaire measures student experiences for the purpose of enhancing admissions procedures. The SAS is a measure of prejudice. It uses experimental and control forms and provides a situational context to make the psychological withdrawal from the stimulus more difficult.

Sedlacek, W.E. 1995. *Improving racial and ethnic diversity and campus climate at four year independent Midwest colleges: An evaluation report of the Lilly Endowment Grant.* College Park: University of Maryland.

This evaluation was designed to encourage and assist institutions in successfully retaining minority students for the full course of the baccalaureate degree. This is an evaluation report of the Lilly Foundation-funded initiatives on thirty campuses. Several direct and indirect changes on campus are attributable to the Lilly initiative, including course revisions, changes in curriculum and library materials, hiring of nontraditional faculty and staff, greater involvement of administration and trustees in diversity issues, ability to train faculty and students on diversity issues, and increased awareness of diversity issues.

Sedlacek, W.E. 1998. Admissions in higher education: Measuring cognitive variables. In D.J. Wilds and R. Wilson, (Eds.). *Sixteenth Annual Status Report on Minorities in Higher Education.* (pp. 47-66) Washington, D.C.: American Council on Education.

Colleges and universities typically use cognitive admissions criteria—high school grade point average, standardized test scores, high school curriculum, and class rank—when determining whom to admit. Noncognitive variables, such as letters of recommendation, extracurricular activities, gender, race/ethnicity, socioeconomic status, leadership ability, and disabilities are also considered by admissions officers, but sometimes to a lesser degree. This essay offers detailed discussion of the literature on assessing success of students of color and examples of traditional and nontraditional admissions criteria. It also sparks discussion and prompts more exploration into how colleges and universities can continue to improve their admissions procedures.

Smith, D.G. 1997. *The Progress of a decade: An imperative for the future. A report to the James Irvine Foundation.* San Francisco, CA.

Since 1987, The James Irvine Foundation has made diversity grants to private colleges and universities throughout California. In the spring of 1996, the Foundation asked Daryl Smith of the Claremont Graduate University to assess the impact of these grants. Dr. Smith, a nationally recognized diversity expert, investigated the changes that have occurred as a result of Irvine's diversity initiatives, focusing specifically on unintended outcomes, lessons learned, the proposal development and evaluation process, and implications for future diversity funding.

Smith, D.G. 1999. Strategic evaluation: An imperative for the future of campus diversity. In M. Cross, N. Cloete, E. Beckham, A. Harper, J. Indiresan, & C. Musil (Eds.) *Diversity and Unity: The role of higher education in building democracy*. (pp. 155-176). Capetown, South Africa: Maskew, Miller, Longman.

Societal changes have forced higher education to think about who it educates, how that education occurs, and how that education impacts the larger society. Creating a pluralistic society often begins with significant diversity; and from that point, the challenge of creating communities that function effectively remains. Increasingly, scholars, from various disciplines, are being expected to develop a new, more diverse knowledge base for higher education and the larger society. This paper outlines some of the issues and progress being made related to the evaluation of emerging campus diversity initiatives.

Smith, D.G., Wolf, L.E., & Levitan, T. (Eds.). 1994. *Studying the diversity in higher education*. *New directions for institutional research*. (No. 81). San Francisco: Jossey Bass.

This volume examines diversity from the point of view of the practicing institutional researcher. Several chapters focus on theoretical issues underlying diversity assessments and methodological questions. Yolanda Moses addresses perceptions of conflict between diversity and institutional excellence, arguing that traditional definitions of excellence are narrow and exclusionary. Antonia Darder makes a case for institutional research as a tool for cultural democracy by explicitly recognizing issues of culture and power. Henry Ingle describes a portfolio system of assessment, Penny Edgert the California Postsecondary Education studies, and Marsha Hirano-Nakanishi a way of framing studies of diversity within the Total Quality Management model. A chapter by the editors on resources, both print and electronic, available to researchers completes the work.

W.K. Kellogg Foundation. 1998. *Evaluation handbook*. Battle Creek, MI: W.K. Kellogg Foundation.

This handbook was initially written for project directors who had direct responsibility for the ongoing evaluation of W.K. Kellogg Foundation funded projects. It provides a framework for thinking about evaluation as a relevant and useful program tool. However, it is a resource for anyone with evaluation responsibilities or interests. Not intended to serve as an exhaustive instructional guide, it provides a framework for thinking about evaluation and outlines a blueprint for designing and conducting evaluations, either independently or with the support of an external evaluator/consultant.

Zúñiga, X., Nagda, B.A., Sevig, T.D., Thompson, M., & Dey, E.L. 1995. *Speaking the unspeakable: Student learning outcomes in intergroup dialogues on a college campus*. Paper presented at the annual meeting if the Association for the Study of Higher Education, November, at Orlando, FL.

The empirical study compared students at the University of Michigan who participated in an intergroup dialogue program with students in related courses including women's studies and sociology. Using pre- and post-assessments of attitudes and values, the study concluded that while the intergroup dialogues were effective, there were differences based on group membership and entering attitudes in the three settings. The study also highlights the kinds of outcomes that can be investigated.


## INTERNET RESOURCES

### DiversityWeb
www.diversityweb.org
DiversityWeb is a collaborative project between the Association of American Colleges and Universities and the University of Maryland, College Park. DiversityWeb is a compendium of promising practices, programs, and resources in higher education that provides online resources on a number of issues regarding diversity in higher education. Its resources are centered around seven campus priorities—Institutional Vision, Leadership and Systemic Change; Student Involvement and Development; Campus and Community Connections; Curriculum Transformation; Faculty and Staff Involvement; Policy and Legal Issues; and Research, Evaluation, and Impact.

### AAHE's Assessment Forum
www.aahe.org/assessment/assessnw.htm
The AAHE Assessment Forum is the primary national network connecting and supporting those involved in higher education assessment. It promotes thoughtful, effective approaches to assessment that involve faculty, benefit students, and improve the quality of teaching and learning. It helps campuses, programs, and individuals to plan, implement, and share the results of their assessment efforts by publishing networking, and sponsoring an annual national conference.

### ERIC Resource on Educational Measurement, Evaluation, Learning Theory

www.ericae.net

Ericae.net is a clearinghouse for assessment, evaluation, and research information. It provides balanced information regarding educational assessment, evaluation, and research methodology, and it provides resources to encourage the responsible use of educational data.

### American Evaluation Association

www.eval.org

The American Evaluation Association is an international professional association of evaluators devoted to the application and exploration of program evaluation, personnel evaluation, technology, and many other forms of evaluation. This website provides information about evaluation practices and methods that could be applicable to a variety of fields.

### Electronic Portfolios for Evaluation

www.aahe.org/teaching/portfolio_db.htm

The Portfolio Clearinghouse, recently acquired from Kalamazoo College, is a searchable collection of portfolio projects from around the world. This database is a tool for institutions researching portfolio programs in use at institutions of higher education and a resource for individuals looking to the portfolio as a means of assessing student learning on the student, faculty, or institutional levels.

### James Irvine Foundation

www.irvine.org

The James Irvine Foundation is a private, nonprofit grant-making foundation dedicated to enhancing the social, economic, and physical quality of life throughout California. Irvine uses evaluation to support philanthropic activity that is better informed, sharper, and more productive. Evaluations of Irvine's program initiatives have provided the first opportunity for the Foundation to determine whether it is meeting its own strategic program goals.

### Practical Assessment, Research, and Evaluation

www.ericae.net/pare

Practical Assessment, Research, and Evaluation is an on-line journal published by the ERIC Clearinghouse on Assessment and Evaluation (ERIC/AE) and the Department of Measurement, Statistics, and Evaluation at the University of Maryland, College Park. Its purpose is to provide education professionals access to articles that can have a positive impact on assessment, research, evaluation and teaching practices.

## Appendix G

# SAMPLE CASE STUDY

### Define the Purpose:

Carnelian University has been working on curriculum transformation for years. The president and board are now interested in understanding the kinds of changes that have been introduced and their impact on student learning.

### Determine the Audience:

The president, board, diversity task force, faculty, and students

### Assemble the Evaluation Team:

Institutional researcher, student affairs staff, member of the diversity task force, academic affairs staff, faculty from different departments

### Identify the Context:

Carnelian University is a campus located in the heart of Philadelphia. It educates a highly diverse, largely commuter, adult population. Its mission statement asserts that "educating a diverse student body for a highly pluralistic society" is one of its central purposes. For years, faculty have been involved in workshops, seminars, and study leaves focusing on new scholarship and curricular change. While students generally feel that they have had an opportunity to engage issues of diversity in the curriculum, some student groups, particularly students of color, are less satisfied in this area.

### Target the topic and formulate the questions:

Using the campus as the unit of analysis, the evaluation seeks to address the following questions:

- How much of the curriculum has been influenced by the transformation efforts, taking into account fields and levels (general education, fields, and majors)?
- How much of the student body has been exposed to these efforts (by groups, fields, etc.)?
- What do we know about the impact of this exposure on student learning?

### *Obtain, Assess, and Analyze Data:*

The evaluation could proceed at a number of levels. One could count the number of faculty and the courses they have worked on to locate the courses that have been changed. A higher level of assessment may focus on course syllabi and observations of selected class sessions. Long-term trends of student responses to a question on the institution's senior survey about exposure to diversity in the curriculum may also provide important data. These data can then be disaggregated by race, ethnicity, gender, major field, etc. A transcript analysis can easily document actual course-taking patterns. Again, these data should be looked at for various groups, fields, courses etc. If examining transcripts for the entire campus is not feasible, doing the analysis on sub-samples (properly developed to allow for the diversity of the campus, fields, etc.) is entirely appropriate and feasible. Enrollments in courses can also be documented.

To evaluate student learning, a number of approaches can be taken. A survey might ask students to self-report how much they have learned in a number of areas and the opportunities they have had to engage issues and people from diverse backgrounds. An assessment might include interviews of students from diverse backgrounds enrolled in courses that emphasize diversity and those that do not. Again, these data need to be looked at in a way that the experiences of different groups of students can be studied. To get at the impact of these experiences on cognitive development, knowledge, attitudes, and perhaps behavior, a campus can select a sample of students and ask for writing samples from those students who have and those who have not experienced much diversity in the curriculum. A team can be established to study the writing and their implications for the campus. A follow-up study of alumni can look at the longer-term impact of the curriculum, including how they feel about the courses taken, what they have learned, and how they have applied what they learned following graduation.

## Report the findings:

As part of a strategic communications plan, evaluators might prepare a written report, presentations to the faculty, student groups, alumni, and board of trustees, and special summary articles for the broader public.

# AAC&U Statement on Liberal Learning

A truly liberal education is one that prepares us to live responsible, productive, and creative lives in a dramatically changing world. It is an education that fosters a well-grounded intellectual resilience, a disposition toward lifelong learning, and an acceptance of responsibility for the ethical consequences of our ideas and actions. Liberal education requires that we understand the foundations of knowledge and inquiry about nature, culture, and society; that we master core skills of perception, analysis, and expression; that we cultivate a respect for truth; that we recognize the importance of historical and cultural context; and that we explore connections among formal learning, citizenship, and service to our communities.

We experience the benefits of liberal learning by pursuing intellectual work that is honest, challenging, and significant, and by preparing ourselves to use knowledge and power in responsible ways. Liberal learning is not confined to particular fields of study. What matters in liberal education is substantial content, rigorous methodology, and an active engagement with the societal, ethical, and practical implications of our learning. The spirit and value of liberal learning are equally relevant to all forms of higher education and to all students.

Because liberal learning aims to free us from the constraints of ignorance, sectarianism, and myopia, it prizes curiosity and seeks to expand the boundaries of human knowledge. By its nature, therefore, liberal learning is global and pluralistic. It embraces the diversity of ideas and experiences that characterize the social, natural, and intellectual world. To acknowledge such diversity in all its forms is both an intellectual commitment and a social responsibility, for nothing less will equip us to understand our world and to pursue fruitful lives.

The ability to think, to learn, and to express oneself both rigorously and creatively, the capacity to understand ideas and issues in context, the commitment to live in society, and the yearning for truth are fundamental features of our humanity. In centering education upon these qualities, liberal learning is society's best investment in our shared future.

*Adopted by the Board of Directors of the Association of American Colleges & Universities, October 1998.* AAC&U encourages distribution, so long as attribution is given. Please address general inquiries to info@aacu.nw.dc.us